P9-CQL-266

# REMEMBER GOLIAD!

# REMEMBER GOLIAD!

*A History of La Bahía*

By Craig H. Roell

TEXAS STATE
HISTORICAL ASSOCIATION

Library of Congress Cataloging-in-Publication Data

Roell, Craig H.
    Remember Goliad! : a history of La Bahía / by Craig H. Roell
    p.      cm.      —(Fred Rider Cotten popular history series ; no. 9)
    Includes bibliographical references.
    ISBN 0-87611-141-X (alk. paper)
    1. Goliad (Tex.)—History. I. Title. II. Series.
    F394.G64R64      1994
    976.4'123—dc20                                                          94-25973
                                                                                  CIP

Number nine in the Fred Rider Cotten Popular History Series.

Published by the Texas State Historical Association in cooperation with the Center
for Studies in Texas History at the University of Texas at Austin.

Cover: Photograph of chapel of Nuestra Señora de Loreto Presidio at Goliad.
*Courtesy Pat Mercer Photography, Victoria.*

# CONTENTS

*To Becky*
*Beloved Sister*

# ACKNOWLEDGMENTS

"I HAVE BEEN CLEARING AWAY BRAMBLES," Stephen F. Austin once wrote, "laying foundations, sowing the seed." An appropriate sentiment also for this project, the harvest of which could not have occurred likewise without the good help of others. I am indebted to my friends and former colleagues at the Texas State Historical Association, especially Ron Tyler, George B. Ward, Douglas Barnett, and Roy R. Barkley. The privilege of working as a staff scholar for two years on the revised *Handbook of Texas* project, South Texas Division, was enormously rewarding to me, an experience indispensable to writing this book. With deepest appreciation I also commend the following for their help: Jack Jackson; John Collins; Cecil Harper Jr.; the archival staffs at the Texas State Archives, the Center for American History, and the Nettie Lee Benson Latin American Collection at the University of Texas at Austin; the Dallas Historical Society; Newton M. Warzecha and staff at Presidio La Bahía, Goliad, Texas, and the Catholic Diocese of Victoria, which owns and operates the presidio; the Texas Department of Parks and Wildlife, especially its staff at Mission La Bahía, Goliad; the Chambers of Commerce, City of Goliad and City of Victoria. The Victoria County Historical Commission provided a forum early in the life of this project. The many authors cited in the Suggested Reading section remain inspirational. Thanks to my parents, I grew up in Victoria, Texas, literally in the middle of the historic area this book describes. Loving gratitude to my mother, Ruth M. Roell, and my father, Henry R. Roell, who provided materials dealing with Goliad. Thanks to my colleagues Frank Saunders and Charlton Moseley in the History Department at Georgia Southern University, Statesboro, for various Georgia sources relating to the Goliad Massacre. Finally, I commend deepest appreciation to my wife, Kay Hendricks Roell—a Georgia girl—and her family for their love and support. The Georgia-Texas connection lives.

# INTRODUCTION

"A 'WILD, RECKY, INDIANY LOOKING PLACE'... full of lawless men [who] would throw the rawhide on to [anyone] in a way that was a pity and a caution." Such was the way a resident described Goliad during the days of the Republic of Texas (1836–1845). Things have calmed down considerably since, but any visitor to this old settlement cannot escape the rich heritage of the area, one of the most historic in the state. Though its population has never exceeded two thousand, Goliad is the largest town in the county of the same name, which was one of the original counties of Texas, created in 1836, and named for the vast territory that was governed as the municipality of Goliad under the Republic of Mexico. Giant oak trees dominate a grassy landscape traditionally given to grazing herds of cattle and horses. The San Antonio River winds slowly from its namesake city through Goliad on its way to San Antonio Bay, a reminder of the venerable link between San Antonio, Goliad, and the Gulf of Mexico.

Though cattle, agribusiness, and oil now provide the economic foundation of the area, tourism is also a vital component. Goliad, situated about a hundred miles south of San Antonio at the intersection of U.S. Highway 59 and U.S. Highways 77A and 183, offers one of the most complete examples of early Texas courthouse squares, which has been named a historic preservation district by the National Register. Besides the town itself, other historic sites include the birthplace of the Mexican patriot Ignacio Zaragoza (hero of Cinco de Mayo), the ruins of the Mission Nuestra Señora del Rosario, and the beautifully restored Mission Nuestra Señora del Espíritu Santo de Zúñiga, a stirring memorial to Goliad's rich Spanish heritage. But the sites that forever etched this sleepy Texas town into the historical consciousness are those made infamous by two of the most controversial episodes of the entire Texas Revolution—the Fannin Battleground at nearby Coleto Creek, and Nuestra Señora de Loreto presidio (popularly called Presidio La Bahía), site of the Goliad Massacre on Palm Sunday, March 27, 1836.

The sad tale of James Walker Fannin and his massacred men became ingrained in Texas folklore, much like the Alamo; unlike the Alamo, quite a few veterans survived Fannin's misfortune, though not all were apparently legitimate. These particular characters warranted comment from Texas's own "Sifter" of tales, Alexander Edwin Sweet (1841-1901). When he published his *On a Mexican Mustang through Texas, From the Gulf to the Rio Grande* in 1883, he included a satirical piece on "The Old Veteran" of the Texas Revolution. "A barbeque without a brigade of veterans is something that has never taken place in Texas," Sweet wrote, describing primarily the *alleged* veteran who, having cornered some patient listeners, would recount once again the pivotal role that he, at least in his own mind, played in that legendary event. Goliad of course had to figure into his story. Sweet slyly captured that tale-teller's boastful art, relating how the old soul claimed to have "received his 'baptism of fire' at San Jacinto or Goliad." Not only did this self-avowed hero pronounce himself "exceedingly intimate with Gen. Sam Houston," but he "boils over with reminiscences of the confidential conversation he had with the father of Texas, 'way back in '36.'" And of course he dourly authored "a modest statement of how different matters would have been if Fannin had only taken the veteran's advice on the morning of the massacre at Goliad." If only, indeed. Such barbeque theatrics have faded with the passing of that particular generation of old veterans, alleged or authentic. Still, Goliad remains fused to the timeless symbol of La Bahía no less than is San Antonio to the Alamo.

Both tragic stories became part of the air Texans breathe. But the same popular historical consciousness that elevated Crockett, Bowie, Travis, Bonham, and their Alamo comrades to heroic proportion has clouded Fannin in mystery and shadow, virtually rechristening his first name to be, "If only. . . ."

La Bahía, literally meaning "the bay," is a term of multiple meanings in Texas history. Various sites on the Gulf Coast were so designated. Spaniards came to use it as an abbreviation for La Bahía del Espíritu Santo, or Bay of the Holy Spirit, now called Matagorda Bay and Lavaca Bay, bounded by present Calhoun, Victoria, Jackson, and Matagorda counties. In 1519 the explorer Alonso Álvarez de Piñeda called the Mississippi River the Río del Espíritu Santo, and others extended the name to the bay. Over time the Spaniards applied the name to a number of locations on the Gulf Coast. The official application of La Bahía del Espíritu Santo, or La Bahía, to mean present Matagorda and Lavaca bays, occurred during the Spanish search to find the rival French colony planted in Texas by René-Robert Cavelier, Sieur de La Salle in 1685.

In Spanish usage, the name La Bahía could refer to the bay itself or to something associated with it. When the viceroy of New Spain authorized expeditions to restore Spanish dominion in Texas following the threat of French encroachment, a detachment of royal soldiers occupied La Bahía del Espíritu Santo (that is, the bay area) in 1721 and founded a presidio (fort), according to official reports, on La Salle's settlement then found in ruins from Indian attacks. The French colony, Fort St. Louis, is generally considered to have been on Garcitas Creek, which empties into the bay. The presidio was named Nuestra Señora Santa María de Loreto de la Bahía del Espíritu Santo, though it was commonly shortened to Nuestra Señora de Loreto, and popularly called simply Presidio La Bahía. When in 1722 the government authorized the founding of a mission near this presidio, it was named Nuestra Señora de la Bahía del Espíritu Santo de Zúñiga, though similarly shortened to Nuestra Señora del Espíritu Santo de Zúñiga, and popularly called simply Mission La Bahía. Thus the bay, as well as the presidio and the mission because of their location on the bay, were all commonly called La Bahía.

Although both mission and presidio La Bahía were at least twice moved farther inland from the bay area, the names, including La Bahía, were retained even when the settlements were permanently relocated on the San Antonio River near what became present-day Goliad and quite far from any bay. Adding to this confusion, the sister missions of Nuestra Señora del Rosario, also near Goliad, and Nuestra Señora del Refugio, near present Refugio, were sometimes grouped with Nuestra Señora del Espíritu Santo and all three called the La Bahía missions. In time a civic settlement grew up around the presidio, and it, too, was known as La Bahía. Located on several important military and trade routes, this village became commercially important. Consequently, La Bahía joined San Antonio de Béxar and Nacogdoches as the three most important areas of Spanish settlement in Texas.

The term La Bahía also had a wider territorial application. Under Spanish government Texas was organized into two vast areas designated as municipalities and named Béxar and La Bahía. Following independence from Spain, the Republic of Mexico created the state of Coahuila y Texas, with Texas itself further divided into three sizable departments by 1834—Béxar, Brazos, and Nacogdoches—with the department of Béxar subdivided into four vast areas called municipalities: San Antonio de Béxar, San Patricio, Guadalupe Victoria, and Goliad. As in the old Spanish system, within the municipalities were villas, or towns, governed by an ayuntamiento, the president of which was called the alcalde, who was the most important person in the municipality.

La Bahía presidio and community continued to be a crucial military and governing center under the Republic of Mexico as the government encouraged Mexican and Anglo-American colonization in Texas. The old settlement was particularly associated with the De León colony at Victoria (the family of Martín De León served in important military and civic positions in La Bahía), the DeWitt colony at Gonzales, and the Power and Hewetson colony at Refugio. It was during this period that the Mexican government promoted the community of La Bahía to a villa—a capital town with municipality jurisdiction—and changed its name to Goliad, a phonetic anagram on the name "Hidalgo" (the Spanish "H" is silent), for Father Miguel Hidalgo y Costilla, a priest commemorated for his part in the Mexican revolution against Spain. Nevertheless, both Mexicans and Anglo-Americans continued to use the old name. Locals came to designate the original settlement and its presidio as "La Bahía" or "old Goliad" while calling the new area of town growing up across the San Antonio River "Goliad."

During the Texas Revolution the town was called both La Bahía and Goliad, though the old Spanish term was used primarily to mean the presidio, and was often corrupted by Anglo-American pronunciation into "Labadee, "Laberdee," "Labaher," or "La Abaia." Control of the old settlement was considered crucial by both sides during the revolution; the fate of Fannin's men was only one episode—albeit the most infamous—in a long series of events. Still, the Goliad Massacre, because of its notoriety and its chronology with the Alamo defeat, supplied one of the two rallying cries heard on the battlefield of San Jacinto, though Sam Houston's army more likely startled Santa Anna's Mexican forces with howls of "Remember the Alamo!" and "Remember Labadee!" than "Remember Goliad!"

During the Republic of Texas and after statehood in 1845 the old La Bahía mission and presidio fell into ruin, but the presidio's military chapel remained intact and was used first as a residence and then for religious services after the Catholic church regained possession about 1855. This chapel became commonly referred to (incorrectly) as "La Bahía Mission," a designation which led to confusion with the actual La Bahía mission, Espíritu Santo, which lay in ruins until reconstructed as a public works project in the 1930s and designated as part of Goliad State Historical Park. The Presidio La Bahía and its chapel were restored in the 1960s by the Kathryn O'Connor Foundation, and is closely associated with the park, though administered under the auspices of the Catholic Diocese of Victoria.

The story of La Bahía encompasses many centuries and cultures. It is an eventful and controversial history. It begins with Spain.

# 1.
# THE SPANISH ERA

*This place affords no advantages as to situation, for good drinking-water is very far off, and timber still farther. The water of the stream is very brackish, so much so that in five days during which the camp was pitched there all the horses sickened.*
— FRAY DAMIÁN MASSANET, DE LEÓN EXPEDITION
SITE OF LA SALLE'S FORT ST. LOUIS, 1689

*These Indians are very dirty and the stench which they emit is enough to turn one's stomach. They are fond of all that is foul and pestiferous and for this reason delight in the odor of the polecat and eat its flesh.*
— FRAY GASPAR JOSÉ DE SOLÍS
INSPECTION OF LA BAHÍA MISSIONS, 1768

THE "GREAT KINGDOM OF THE TEXAS." So did early Spanish explorers christen the vast northern frontier of New Spain, named for the ancient Indian greeting *"techas"* or *"tejas,"* meaning "friends" or "allies," and applied by the Spaniards to the whole region and its inhabitants. But this so-called "land of the friends" became pivotal in the New World contest of empires between Spain and France. This rivalry intensified in the Texas wilderness in the late seventeenth and early eighteenth centuries following the establishment of Fort St. Louis, the first French colony in Texas, by René-Robert

Cavelier, Sieur de La Salle. The French explorer founded his settlement near the shores of La Bahía del Espíritu Santo (Bay of the Holy Spirit) in 1685. The Spaniards launched five sea voyages and six land marches to find the intruders. Finally, on April 22, 1689, an expedition under Alonso de León, accompanied by the missionary Fray Damián Massanet, discovered the somber ruins of the ill-fated French colony; La Salle's venture was unsuccessful and ended in death for him and most of his 280 settlers and soldiers, victims of the wilderness, Indians, disease, and mutiny. Nevertheless, the possibility of French claims on the region inspired Spain to establish a system of missions and presidios as part of a formidable plan to colonize the area, encourage and protect trade routes, and Christianize native inhabitants. Among the many outposts that the Spaniards established, two would prove crucial in future events. In 1718 Martín de Alarcón, governor of the provinces of Coahuila and Texas, founded San Antonio de Béxar presidio and San Antonio de Valero mission (whose chapel would popularly be called the Alamo), laying the foundation for what became the foremost settlement in Spanish Texas.

A separate expedition three years later led by the Marqués de San Miguel de Aguayo, then governor and captain-general of Coahuila and Texas, was sent to establish the second pivotal settlement, La Bahía, literally on the ashes of La Salle's French colony. According to official reports, Espíritu Santo Bay was secured on April 4, 1721, by Aguayo's advance unit under Capt. Domingo Ramón, who then founded Presidio Nuestra Señora de Loreto on the ruins of Fort St. Louis. Aguayo arrived in April 1722 and began construction on a permanent fortification. Archaeological evidence confirms that this site was on the west bank of Garcitas Creek about two miles above its mouth on Lavaca Bay in present Victoria County. The name of this presidio, which formally appears in Spanish records as Nuestra Señora Santa María de Loreto de la Bahía del Espíritu Santo, honored the shrine of Holy House of the Virgin of Nazareth located in Loreto, Italy, and referred as well to the presidio's location on the Bay of the Holy Spirit.

Nuestra Señora del Espíritu Santo de Zúñiga Mission, Goliad (restoration). *Courtesy Texas Department of Transportation.*

Aguayo authorized Father Agustín Patrón y Guzmán to establish the nearby mission, Nuestra Señora del Espíritu Santo de Zúñiga, among the area's Karankawan tribes (the Coco, Cujane, Copane, and Karankawa proper). The name of this mission, which formally appears in Spanish records as Nuestra Señora de la Bahía del Espíritu Santo de Zúñiga, was a reference to its bay location and also honored the viceroy of New Spain, Baltasar de Zúñiga y Guzmán, Marqués de Valero. Espíritu Santo, which was to become one of the most successful missions in Texas, was placed in the care of the Franciscan missionaries from the college of Nuestra Señora de Guadalupe de Zacatecas.

However strategic to prevent French aggression, and despite its natural beauty, the Garcitas Creek site proved a hostile, unhealthy environment. The humid sub-tropical climate and wet surroundings enlivened a pesky mosquito population, which was to be acknowledged in the names given to local creeks and bayous. Alligators infested the waters, many buffalo grazed the swampy grasslands, and salt-water lagoons dotted a landscape that Fray Massanet had criticized as affording "no advantages as to situation, for good drinking-water is very far off, and timber still farther. The water of the stream is very brackish, so much so that in five days during which the camp was pitched there all the horses sickened."

And yet it was the various Karankawan tribes of the area that offered the most challenge, as La Salle's colony had tragically discovered. Ferocious, nomadic, and primitive, reeking from their diet and personal habits (which included smearing themselves with fetid fish or alligator oil and skunk musk to ward off bothersome mosquitoes), they offended Spanish senses of smell and notions of a civilized life. "They are fond of all that is foul and pestiferous," Fray Gaspar José de Solís recorded, "and for this reason delight in the odor of the polecat and eat its flesh." They were given to thievery and violence, including ritualistic cannibalism reserved for captured foes. Fray Solís described Karankawan culture in great detail, including their controversial cannibalism. During a lavish dancing and musical ritual called the *mitote*, "they draw near to the victim, cut off a piece of his flesh, come to the fire and half roast it, and within sight of the victim himself devour it most ravenously. Thus they continue cutting him to pieces and dismembering him, until, finally, they have cut away all of his flesh and he dies...." To the undaunted missionaries, these Indians seemed prime candidates for bringing into the Holy Church. But the task proved extraordinarily difficult. As Fray Solís wrote as late as 1768, "they are anxious to be free from all servitude and from work and wish to return to their life of freedom and idleness. They have, moreover, a repugnance and distaste for the teachings of our holy faith and for the things of God, and they are loathe to observe our holy commandments and sovereign precepts."

In April 1722, at about the same time that Mission Espíritu Santo was founded, the permanent structure for Presidio Nuestra Señora de Loreto began to take shape. A surviving plan shows that the completed fort was to be octagon shaped with a moat, four bastions, and a tower. Aguayo left Capt. Domingo Ramón in command of the garrison of forty soldiers, which was later reinforced with fifty men from San Antonio de Béxar. But Ramón was unable to keep the garrison disciplined; antagonism and hostilities with the Karankawan tribes resulted and Ramón was killed. His son, Diego Ramón III, then became presidio captain, but was removed for inefficiency and replaced by an adept and talented administrator, Juan Antonio Bustillo y Zevallos.[1] Under his able direction, and that of his successors, Nuestra Señora de Loreto achieved preeminence among all Texas presidios.

Unable to induce the nomadic Karankawan tribes to accept Catholic teachings or even stay at the mission, the Franciscan padres as early as April 1725 recommended moving the mission and its presidio to a location more favorable to their missionary efforts, a measure also prompted by continuing incidents of ill feeling and violence between these Indians and the presidio soldiers. By April 1726 both mission and presidio La Bahía had been relocated about ten leagues west (some twenty-six miles inland) among the more amenable Aranama and Tamique tribes at a site on the Guadalupe River now called Mission Valley in present Victoria County.

Here among ancient oak and pecan trees the reputation and importance of La Bahía would blossom. Its new and satisfying location among tribes that were agricultural, sedentary, and friendly greatly inspired the missionaries. The Guadalupe River setting was most pleasing, its climate considerably more healthy, its grassy plains conducive to stock grazing and farming (though trees were also in abundance), and a stone quarry was available ten leagues away. As Fray Massanet had recorded in 1689, "The country was the most pleasant that we have traversed" and the river banks "are covered with timber." At least two dams were constructed within a five-mile radius of the mission to direct water from the Guadalupe River and a tributary, Mission Creek, through stone irrigation ditches into fields for crop cultivation. But the padres soon found that normal rainfall was adequate. On the Guadalupe some twelve miles downriver, on a bluff called Tonkawa Bank near a popular low water crossing, the mission's associated ranchería (small village)—or possibly its visita (country

VIEW OF THE RUINS OF THE OLD CHURCH AND FORTIFICATION AT GOLIAD.

Engraving, *View of the Ruins of the Old Church and Fortification at Goliad*, from George C. Furber's *The Twelve Months Volunteer, or, Journal of a Private, in the Tennessee Regiment of Cavalry, in the Campaign in Mexico, 1846–7* (Cincinnati: J. A. and U. P. James, 1848).

chapel)—was constructed. (This site, identified by a state historical marker, is in Riverside Park in Victoria, Texas.)

For the next twenty-three years at the Mission Valley location the La Bahía mission and presidio prospered in both agricultural and missionary pursuits. Successful farming and cattle ranching enabled these Spaniards, with the aid of Indian wards, to supply themselves as well as other Texas missions and settlements with ample food. The main industry was livestock raising and export-ing, particularly cattle and horses, which already grazed and roamed on the prairies bordered by the Guadalupe and Lavaca rivers on the north and the San Antonio River on the south. This endeavor laid the foundation for what became one of the charac-teristic industries of Texas—livestock ranching. Future Mexican and Anglo-American ranchers of Texas would build fortunes from the thousands of Longhorn cattle and mustang horses descended from these estrayed La Bahía herds. Texas braggadocio to the con-trary, it is no exaggeration to say that the cradle of the Western

Nuestra Señora de Loreto Presidio, Goliad (restoration). *Courtesy Texas Department of Transportation.*

cattle industry lay in the grassland prairie of La Bahía at its Mission Valley site.

The Spanish royal government, ever concerned about halting French and eventually English encroachment on its North American domain, authorized an expedition under José de Escandón to evaluate the northern frontier. In early 1747 Escandón ordered a reconnaissance of South Texas by the captain of Presidio La Bahía, Joaquín Prudencio de Orobio y Basterra. Based on Orobio's reports Escandón recommended moving the La Bahía presidio and mission, despite their success and favorable location, from the Guadalupe to the San Antonio River as a strategic move to better protect settlements on the lower Río Grande. The proposed site was similarly suited to crop and stock raising, and timber, stone, lime, and other building materials were plentiful. Likewise, missionary efforts were similarly expected to produce success among area tribes.

Escandón, who was made governor and captain general of Nuevo Santander in 1749, is called the "Father of Goliad." Acting on his proposals, the Spanish viceroy soon ordered the mission and presidio moved to his recommended location, a place Orobio had named Santa Dorotea (St. Dorothy). Having to abandon so successful and rewarding a site proved to be a sad experience. The move from the Guadalupe to the San Antonio River occurred in the fall of 1749, probably in October, since a government report dated November 16, 1749, shows the removal had been accomplished. This would be mission and presidio La Bahía's permanent location. Orobio was charged with the task, and despite being denied extra assistance by the government, managed to traverse the creeks and wooded prairies with ox carts and mules. Escandón planned to settle twenty-five northern Mexican families from Nuevo León or Coahuila at the Santa Dorotea site, but this failed to materialize. Nevertheless, a civilian community would eventually develop to complement the missionary and military settlement. In these were the roots of Goliad.

Four months after this move the presidio, now under the command of Capt. Manuel Ramírez de la Piszena, consisted of a large barracks and forty temporary houses built of wood and caliche mud for the garrison soldiers and their families; the captain's house of several rooms built of stone at his own expense for emergency protection; and a roomy chapel. The garrison was well armed, including six 8-pounder cannon, and numbered fifty men, who were stationed not only at the presidio, but also at nearby Mission Espíritu Santo—and, after 1754, at neighboring Mission Nuestra Señora del Rosario.[2] Some of these soldiers also were detailed to guard La Bahía's herd of horses pastured several leagues downriver and escort the convoys and supply trains from San Antonio and the Rio Grande. These essential soldiers became crucial as Lipan Apache Indians increasingly raided the area by the mid-1750s. Among the children born to these royal soldiers of La Bahía were future Mexican patriot Carlos de la Garza, a key figure in the Goliad campaign during the Texas Revolution, and Ignacio Zaragoza, who would achieve heroic fame as leader of the

Mexican forces that defeated the French at Puebla on May 5, 1862 (Cinco de Mayo).

Under Capt. Ramírez's direction, permanent structures were built at La Bahía presidio and mission, and at Mission Rosario as part of the government's plan to better defend its expanding frontier. As a result of the Peace of Paris in February 1763, which ended the terribly expensive Seven Years' War, France had to transfer all of its vast Louisiana territory to Spain, a monumental increase in Spanish land holdings in North America. Texas, long the Spanish hinterland, was now sandwiched between Coahuila and the new buffer zone that extended to the Mississippi River and included the city of New Orleans. As a result, the Spanish government ordered an incredible eight thousand-mile inspection of the northern frontier from the Gulf of California to the Louisiana border at Los Adaes. Its goals—to redetermine governing policies of both old and new territories, to insure protection against threats by the Indians, English, French, and even Russians, and yet find ways to economize in order to help eliminate the critically severe Spanish national debt resulting from the Seven Years' War.

During 1767, Texas was examined by the Marqués de Rubí (Cayetano María Pignatelli Rubí Corbera y San Clement). His tour convinced him that Spanish success in Texas was greatly at risk and required concentrating on practical and strategic settlements while eliminating isolated or useless ones. His recommendations, known as the "New Regulations of the Presidios,"[3] called for advancing San Antonio and La Bahía (including Mission Rosario) to preeminence, but temporarily abandoning most other establishments. By royal order East Texas was abandoned (until Nacogdoches was resettled in 1779), while Presidio La Bahía was rebuilt of stone and remained the only Spanish fortress for the entire Gulf Coast from the mouth of the Rio Grande to the Mississippi River. Located on major trade and military routes, La Bahía also grew in commercial importance, becoming one of three crucial areas of Spanish settlement in Texas, along with San Antonio and Nacogdoches.

On at least two occasions—in 1769 and 1771—the La Bahía garrison thwarted French and English intruders. During the American Revolution, soldiers from the presidio assisted Spanish armies of Gen. Bernardo de Gálvez in victories over the British in Louisiana and Florida from 1779–1782. Gálvez's energetic assistance toward American independence established a friendly relationship between the new nation and Mexico that would soon be replaced with a fear of the fast-growing United States. Still, the Texas port of Galveston honors his name and memory.

Like its presidio, when Mission Espíritu Santo was moved from the Guadalupe to the San Antonio River site, it was first constructed of wood and caliche mud. But by 1758 Father Francisco Xavier de Salazar was able to report to Governor Jacinto de Barrios y Jáuregui that the mission complex had been rebuilt of stone and mortar, though the mission's Indian population (which in May 1758 was 49 warriors, 50 women, and 79 children) was still living in primitive *jacales*. The missionaries tried to use a manual of Coahuiltecan words compiled in 1760 by Father Bartolome García of Mission San Francisco de la Espada to communicate with these people because of difficulties with teaching them in Spanish.

Here on the San Antonio River the resourceful padres of Espíritu Santo focused their missionary work primarily among the Aranama and Tamique Indians who had followed from the Guadalupe River location. The missionaries had less success among the new area's Tonkawa and Karankawan tribes. Desertion and tribal rivalry remained problematic. Further, Lipan Apaches increasingly preyed upon the mission's cattle and inhabitants, but Espíritu Santo still prospered. During his official inspection tour of the Zacatecan missions in 1767–1768, Gaspar José de Solís recorded that Espíritu Santo was smaller but in better condition than its nearby sister mission, Nuestra Señora del Rosario. The royal presidio at La Bahía was within sight of Espíritu Santo across the San Antonio River, which was crossed by canoe and had a large stock of fish. Fray Solís complimented the sole priest's zeal in ministering to and educating the Indians as well as the presidio soldiers. He noted large herds of cattle, horses, mules, oxen, and sheep, and cropland yielding corn, cotton, melons, potatoes,

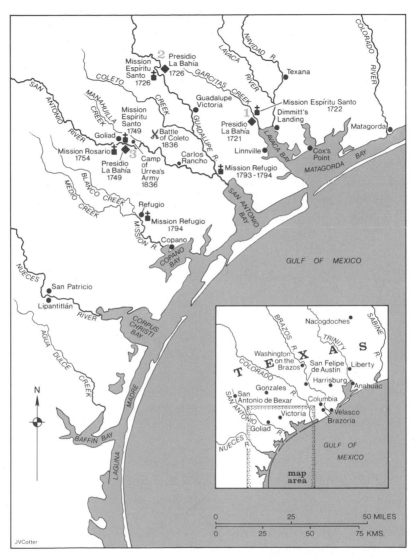

Texas Gulf Coast, 1835–1836.

peaches, and figs. Espíritu Santo's population, including
Aranamas, Tamiques, Piguique, and Manos de Perro Indians,[4]

numbered some three hundred, he recorded, and since the mission's founding in 1722 there had been 623 baptisms and 278 burials.

Espíritu Santo is traditionally recognized as the first great cattle ranch in Texas. Historians estimate the total number of Longhorn cattle belonging to the mission to have reached some 40,000, with those actually branded in 1778 numbering over 15,000 head. When Mission Rosario was temporarily abandoned in 1779 and again in 1781, its herds of cattle were also combined with those of Espíritu Santo. The hardy Longhorns were a dependable source of food and the mission's major source of wealth. These herds were driven by Spanish and Indian cowhands to other missions and to Mexico and Louisiana and exchanged for corn and other needed supplies. Between May and September of 1780 alone at least 4,700 head were trailed to Louisiana from La Bahía. The incredible number of wild Longhorns and mustangs in Texas led many profit-motivated Spaniards to capture these animals for such drives, despite having to pay license and export fees for each animal. Thus did the legendary ranching industry begin, and with it the tales of two preeminently Texas beasts.

By the 1790s conditions at both Mission Espíritu Santo and Presidio La Bahía had deteriorated, however. A terrifying cholera epidemic occurred in 1780. Clashes between the various tribes who visited the mission complex increased, as did raids by fearsome Karankawa, Lipan Apache, and Comanche Indians. Too few soldiers at the presidio were unable to protect the mission settlement adequately. The Spanish royal government's lack of understanding of conditions in the Interior Provinces led to the passage of unsatisfactory and injurious policies. Espíritu Santo, like all Texas missions, was not intended to be a permanent institution. With the Secularization Decree of April 10, 1794, the Spanish government declared that the padres had accomplished their purpose; the mission property and land were to be distributed among the Indian converts, and the church turned over to secular clergy. Governor Manuel Muñoz petitioned the royal government for a five-year extension for Espíritu Santo, as well as for the nearby Rosario and Refugio missions, believing that the Indians here were incapable of managing their own affairs. Authorities in Mexico granted the request on May 10, 1797, though internal turmoil in the government allowed an even longer extension. Indeed, the various decrees of secularization issued from Spain from 1793 to 1813 seem hardly to have affected Mission La Bahía.

Although Presidio La Bahía also had become run-down by the 1790s, repairs were authorized by the Spanish government. Still of strategic importance in guarding major roads, especially as Indian attacks increased (primarily by Lipan Apache and Comanche tribes), the old fort took on new priority with the completion in 1795 of Mission Nuestra Señora del Refugio twenty-seven miles to the southwest on Mission River near present Refugio.[5] In addition, the civic settlement of La Bahía continued to grow near the presidio, which by 1804 could boast having one of two schools operating in Texas (the other was at San Antonio). As political unrest in Mexico against Spain at this time exploded in local episodes of revolt, the presidio's significance was additionally underscored, especially during the 1810 insurrection of Father Hidalgo, the Gutiérrez-Magee Expedition of 1812–1813, and the campaigns of Henry Perry in 1817 and James Long in 1821. In part a consequence of the purchase of Louisiana by the Jefferson administration in 1803, much of this agitation involved adventurers and nationalists from the United States who saw Texas as an opportunity for American expansionism. Whether because of widespread Mexican revolutionary unrest against the royal Spanish government, or local concern about Indian attack, or filibuster attempts to "Americanize" Texas, La Bahía would indeed become an unusually busy place.

Although the revolt against the Spanish government that was inspired by Padre Miguel Hidalgo y Costilla (popularly known as Father Hidalgo) on September 16, 1810, occurred in interior Mexico, its repercussions spread to Texas. Revolutionists in San Antonio de Béxar under Juan Bautista de las Casas led the movement and pressured La Bahía to follow suit. Success was limited and short-lived. Some loyalists unwilling to renounce royal Spanish authority, which included La Bahía's presidio commander, were forced to flee to Coahuila. Others, such as the presidio's chaplain, Father Miguel Martínez, stayed to inspire the citizens of the budding village of La Bahía to oppose the revolution. The divided and frightened community was restored after the Casas Revolution was crushed by Juan Manuel Zambrano and Father Hidalgo's insurrection was defeated in Mexico; Zambrano would even establish a nonmission school for families of soldiers and settlers at La Bahía in 1818. But Hidalgo's valiant efforts would not be forgotten, for his name would later provide the phonetic anagram for the future name of the settlement, "Goliad." (Mexican sources occasionally render the spelling "Golhiad," thus including the silent "H" in the anagram.)

During the Hidalgo revolt rebels loyal to the padre's cause recruited José Bernardo Gutiérrez de Lara to secure help in the United States, a mission that he continued even after Hidalgo's capture. Although the U.S. secretary of State, James Monroe, and other officials in Washington, D.C., made only vague promises, Gutiérrez was able to organize an expedition in New Orleans and Natchitoches, Louisiana, with adventurers who hoped to liberate Texas as an independent republic or even win it for the United States. Among them was Augustus W. Magee, a disaffected U.S. Army officer who helped Gutiérrez assemble the campaign with American, Mexican, and even French volunteers. The expedition set out in April 1812 with perhaps as many as 700 men determined to capture the strategic centers of San Antonio and La Bahía. The latter was taken virtually without contest in early November because the Spanish governor of Texas, Manuel María de Salcedo, had ordered much of the La Bahía garrison away to reinforce San Antonio. The invaders victoriously hoisted the so-called "Green Flag of the First Republic of the North" above the presidio walls. Finding supplies, munitions, and cannon, they settled in to await the Spanish response.

The wait was brief. Royal troops from San Antonio led by Governor Salcedo and Gen. Simón de Herrera established a headquarters across the river at Mission Espíritu Santo and began siege of the presidio on November 13. The controversial episode lasted about four months, during which time various sorties were interrupted with periods of calm. Magee died on February 6, apparently a suicide. On February 10 and 13, the filibusters under their new commander, Samuel Kemper, defeated Salcedo's force, which then retreated toward San Antonio. Kemper and Gutiérrez pursued them, reportedly with mission Indians, again defeating Salcedo and Herrera near San Antonio on March 29. Though the Gutiérrez insurrection would achieve additional victories (and notoriety, for it executed Salcedo, Herrera, and other prominent Spanish leaders), ultimately the royalists under Joaquín de Arredondo defeated the movement at the battle of the Medina River on August 18, 1813.

La Bahía returned to royalist control in July or August 1813, though the settlement suffered during Arredondo's vengeful policy of purging Texas of all foreigners and revolutionaries. Commander Luciano García was sent to bring the La Bahía garrison to its full complement as specified under the Marqués de Rubí's "Regulations for the Presidios" of 1772. But this respite was short-lived. An American, Henry Perry, who was an officer in the Gutiérrez-Magee expedition and a participant in the 1812–1813 siege of La Bahía, returned to Texas in 1817 in yet another independence scheme. That June the strategic settlement found itself again in battle when Perry tried to capture the old presidio. Its garrison, reinforced by royal soldiers from San Antonio under Governor Antonio María Martínez, defeated Perry's band of some fifty men on June 18 in the vicinity of nearby Coleto Creek. All but four of the invaders were killed or captured (Perry himself committed suicide), a number of presidio officers and men were killed, as was one citizen of La Bahía village. Secure in this royalist victory, the presidio, mission, and village then returned, albeit temporarily, to normal life.

Although threats from foreign encroachment were certainly not new to a Spanish Texas long watchful against the French, English, Karankawan, Lipan Apache, and Comanche Indian tribes, the American filibusters arguably posed the most serious challenge. Dating at least to the exploits of Philip Nolan,[6] the American threat was exacerbated by increasing Mexican republican agitation against royal rule inspired by the American and French revolutions. Furthermore, France under Napoleon regained Spanish

William Bollaert's drawing, *Goliad*, ca. 1843. *Courtesy Edward Ayer Collection, Newberry Library, Chicago.*

Louisiana and New Orleans only to sell them to the United States in 1803—President Thomas Jefferson's enlightened (and strategic) "Louisiana Purchase." The exact boundary between Spanish Texas and this new American Louisiana was a matter of considerable debate heightened still further by a popular American attitude that believed that much of Texas was part of the Louisiana Purchase anyway—a claim based on French acceptance of La Salle's colonization efforts so long before.

Spanish fears, which inevitably alerted the garrison at La Bahía, resulted from such seemingly innocent moves as President Jefferson's attempt in 1804–1806 to investigate the Red River area. More legitimate apprehensions were aroused by the mysterious maneuvers of Jefferson's former vice president, Aaron Burr, who conspired with U.S. Gen. James Wilkinson to invade Texas as part of a plan to take over Spain's North American colonies. The Gutiérrez-Magee, Kemper, and Perry episodes confirmed Spanish suspicions. These fears were somewhat abated in 1819 by the Adams-Onís Treaty between the United States and Spain, which renounced the American claim to Texas. But La Bahía was soon brought directly into the Spanish-American conflict again with a filibuster attempt by James Long, a resident of Natchez, Mississippi, upset with the Adams-Onís Treaty, who helped organize an expedition to conquer Texas in 1819. Though aided by Mexican insurrectionists, notably including the veteran José Bernardo Gutiérrez de Lara, Long was expelled from Nacogdoches by royal Spanish troops under Col. Ignacio Pérez.

Still allied with Gutiérrez, Long tried again in October 1821, seven months after Mexico had declared its independence from Spain. La Bahía was naturally a strategic target. Long's force of 52 men landed on the west bank of the Guadalupe River and marched overland to La Bahía. The presidio was surprised and easily captured on October 4. Four days later reinforcements, again under Col. Pérez, arrived unexpectedly from San Antonio and, headquartered at Mission Espíritu Santo, fired shots and shells into the presidio from the house tops of La Bahía village. Eventually, Long surrendered to Pérez. The Americans were first imprisoned in San Antonio and later in Mexico City, where Long was killed under suspicious circumstances.

Meanwhile, at La Bahía, presidio commander Tomás Buentello served as alcalde of the village under the auspices of the newly independent Republic of Mexico. The old settlement would soon find new purpose aligned with the efforts encouraged by Mexico City to colonize Texas with Mexicans and acceptable foreigners, a policy designed to protect this northernmost province of Mexico from further encroachment by the United States.

# 2.
# EMPRESARIOS

*Inasmuch as the principal object of the Nation, is to establish peaceful relations, and settle the uncultivated lands and uninhabited wilds of Texas . . . and above all afford the means of enlightenment and a knowledge of the Divinity of the Lord our God . . . I therefore pray your Excellencies . . . to grant me permission to found a town . . . on the Guadalupe River at a distance of about ten leagues beyond La Bahía del Espíritu Santo.*
—MARTÍN DE LEÓN, PETITION FOR THE FOUNDING OF
GUADALUPE VICTORIA, APRIL 8, 1824

*That, this resolution be made known to the Empresario Green DeWitt, in order that he may not in any manner whatever molest the inhabitants of the town of Guadalupe de Victoria, nor interfere with the progress of their building of farming.*
—ORDER AND DECREE OF THE GOVERNOR
STATE OF COAHUILA Y TEXAS, OCTOBER 6, 1825

"MEXICO HAD DECLARED HER INDEPENDENCE of Spain; . . . Stephen F. Austin had securely planted his colony on the Brazos River, and Americans had gained a footing on Texan soil which they were destined never more to relinquish," wrote John J. Linn, an Irish immigrant himself destined to become a leader in De León's

Colony and in the Texas Revolution against Mexico. "In travelling from Corpus Christi to Victoria I was delighted with the appearance of the country. It was in the last days of April and the landscape was rendered charming by the profusion of many-colored wild flowers that greeted the eye on all sides." Linn settled in Victoria in 1829, became its alcalde in 1836, and like his fellow colonists, would soon be pulled into the strong orbit of La Bahía.

Ever concerned that the province of Texas would become absorbed into the United States through filibuster campaigns, the new government of the Republic of Mexico, following a prescription initiated in the last years of the Spanish regime, actively encouraged the colonization of Texas with "favored" people— Mexicans, Irish, and Anglo-Americans professing to be good and moral Catholics. Ironically, from these same people came the movement to make Texas a Mexican state separate from Coahuila, which would lead eventually to the effort to make Texas independent of Mexico altogether. A variety of ambitious men called empresarios led settlers into Texas under the auspices of several colonization laws. Had their contracts been successfully fulfilled— most were not by far—over nine thousand families would have been brought into the province. Preeminent among these empresarios were Moses and Stephen F. Austin, whose distant colony only indirectly affected La Bahía. Rather, the crucial old presidial settlement was much more a center for the predominantly Mexican colony of Martín De León, the Anglo-American colony of Green DeWitt, and the two Irish colonies: McMullen and McGloin, and Power and Hewetson.

Under the Mexican government, Presidio La Bahía served as a military fortress for the protection and supervision of these colonies. By October 1824 Martín De León founded Nuestra Señora de Guadalupe de Jesús Victoria on the Guadalupe River at El Sabinal (Cypress Grove), thought to be the site where the river was discovered by Alonso de León, who had named the watercourse in 1689 after the Virgin of Guadalupe (patron saint of Mexico). The empresario named his settlement to honor the Virgin, and also his friend, Guadalupe Victoria (Juan Félix Fernández), the first president of the Republic of Mexico and hero

(Left) Portrait of empresario Don Martín De León by John Hobby Jr. based on information supplied by the De León family. *Courtesy Texian Press, Waco.* (Right) John J. (Juan) Linn, engraving, frontispiece of Linn's *Reminiscences of Fifty Years in Texas* (1883). *Courtesy Center for American History, University of Texas at Austin.*

of the revolution. Indeed, the colony was popularly called simply Guadalupe Victoria. Texas attracted Martín De León, a rancher in Nuevo Santander (now Tamaulipas), after he visited La Bahía, San Antonio, and Nacogdoches in 1805. He established ranches first on the Aransas River and later on the Nueces River near present San Patricio, and soon was driving livestock to market at New Orleans—cattle and horses descended from the old La Bahía herds and captured in the wild. De León was a republican supporter against the royalists, and after Mexico won independence from Spain, he took advantage of the more liberal colonization policy of the new government. His grant to settle forty-one Mexican families "of good moral character" on the lower Guadalupe River "at a distance of about ten leagues beyond La Bahía del Espíritu Santo" was approved on April 13, 1824.

De León's Colony was the only predominantly Mexican colony in Texas, augmented by a few Anglo-American and Irish families.

Notably included was John J. Linn, who would establish a port called Linnville on Lavaca Bay to take advantage of Guadalupe Victoria's growing importance in commercial trade. As a Mexican citizen of aristocratic birth, De León received legal preference in the numerous border disputes with the Anglo settlements that would encircle Guadalupe Victoria (present Victoria). Compelling and influential both as empresario and first alcalde, he stood six feet tall and was skilled as a horseman and Indian fighter; Indians called him *"Capitán Vaca Mucha"* ("Captain Plenty of Cows") since he often placated raiding parties by feeding them beef. His five-league (22,140-acre) ranch was located in what became southeastern Victoria County on Garcitas Creek and probably included the site of La Salle's Fort St. Louis and the original location of presidio and mission La Bahía. His thousands of cattle were branded with an E and J connected, signifying "Espíritu de Jesús"—said to have been the brand of the royal family of Spain and the oldest in Texas.

As neighboring settlements having the same culture and religion, La Bahía and De León's Colony became naturally associated. But the ties were even stronger. In addition to dominating Guadalupe Victoria, the family of Martín De León controlled the ayuntamiento of Goliad—sons-in-law José Miguel Aldrete and Rafael Manchola were alcaldes, and Manchola also served as commandant of the La Bahía garrison. Furthermore, Manchola was one of the esteemed "Ten Friends" designated in the name of Guadalupe Victoria's main street, *Calle de los Díez Amigos*, which implied the unity of the principal citizens entrusted with the colony's welfare. Manchola, who was a resident of La Bahía and served as the Texas deputy in the congress of Coahuila y Texas, would be instrumental in the name change from La Bahía to Goliad. Aldrete, who was probably born at La Bahía, also was tax collector of the nearby port of Copano, land commissioner of Coahuila y Texas, as well as commissioner general to the Power and Hewetson Colony. De León's other sons and sons-in-law were primarily involved in the affairs of Guadalupe Victoria as members of the "Ten Friends": Fernando De León was the colonization commissioner, Silvestre De León was second alcalde, José M. J.

Carbajal was surveyor-engineer of the colony, and Plácido Benavides was militia captain and third alcalde. All of these men—together with John J. Linn—operated in the La Bahía-Guadalupe Victoria orbit and would become crucial (though sadly forgotten) protagonists in the Texas Revolution.

Empresario Green DeWitt, stirred by Austin's accomplishment, established his colony in 1825, traditionally considered the most successful of the Anglo-American settlements in Texas next to Austin's. Indeed, Austin's influence helped DeWitt secure permission from the Mexican government on April 15, 1825, to settle "four hundred industrious Catholic families . . . known to be respectable," and any Mexican families of similar character who "shall come to settle with us." Born in Kentucky in 1787, DeWitt grew up in that part of Spanish-held Louisiana territory that would be known as Missouri. After Missouri Territory became part of the United States with the Louisiana Purchase, he served in the state militia during the War of 1812 and later in Missouri politics before being inspired by Austin (also a noted Missouri politician) to come to Texas.

DeWitt's colony was to be on the Guadalupe, San Marcos, and Lavaca Rivers adjacent to and southwest of Austin's grant and subject to the Colonization Law of 1824. He was said by a contemporary to be "as enthusiastic in praise of the country as the most energetic real estate dealer of boom towns nowadays." He worked closely with his surveyor James Kerr to develop the settlement. DeWitt apparently did not enjoy the degree of personal influence over his settlement that Austin exercised at San Felipe, or De León at Guadalupe Victoria, for he never held an elected office in the colony's government. Unlike Austin or De León, he was unable to fulfill his colonization contract by the time it expired on April 15, 1831, and he failed to get it renewed.

James Kerr chose the site for the new colony's capital at the junction of the Guadalupe and San Marcos rivers. Despite being hampered by Indians, he then drew plans for the new town, naming it Gonzales to honor the provisional governor of Coahuila y Texas, Rafael Gonzáles. Settlers began arriving in the summer of 1825. DeWitt himself visited the budding colony in October, but returned to Missouri to promote his enterprise. In July 1826 Indians attacked the infant settlement on a horse-stealing raid, causing many to flee north to Austin's colony on the Colorado River. Gonzales's vulnerability induced Kerr to find another site nearer the coast. With the permission of the Mexican government in San Antonio, he established "Old Station" near the mouth of the Lavaca River at Matagorda Bay as a landing point for colonists under the condition that the settlement remain temporary until enough colonists gathered to insure the safety of Gonzales (the colonization law forbid any permanent settlement within ten leagues of the coast).

By October 1826 the population of Old Station had grown to some forty people, including DeWitt's own family. Rude cabins were built and crops planted, and though no land grants could be issued in this forbidden zone, Old Station was granted a temporary alcalde. Harsh living conditions were exacerbated by the area's unfriendly Karankawan tribes. But the greatest challenge came from Martín De León. The legislature of Coahuila y Texas inadvertently included De León's Colony within the boundaries of the grant made to DeWitt. De León resented being encircled by Anglo-American colonists, and the establishment of Old Station was particularly unwelcome. As an influential Mexican citizen De León received preference in the ensuing legal battle over boundaries, especially because DeWitt's contract, which was issued after De León's, required the American to respect the rights of previous settlers. Furthermore, despite its colonization program the Mexican government was growing distrustful of all foreigners and therefore was quite suspicious that DeWitt settlers were engaged in contraband trade and were trying to relocate the colony in the forbidden zone. Official communications from the Mexican government not only distinguished between "the foreigner Green De Witt" and "the justice of [De León's] pretension," but ordered that the American "may not in any manner whatever molest the inhabitants of the town of Guadalupe de Victoria, nor interfere with the progress of their building or farming."

Relations between the two colonies further deteriorated in October 1826. The schooner *Escambia* arrived at the mouth of the

Lavaca River with merchandise for trade, which included contraband tobacco. Upon discovering the infraction, the jefe político (political chief) at San Antonio ordered De León, with the aid of the La Bahía presidio garrison under command of his son-in-law, Rafael Manchola, to seize the contraband. Rumors spread that De León and Manchola were allying with Indians to kill Anglo-American settlers as far as the Colorado River, and that the Mexican empresario would return with DeWitt's head tied to his saddle. With little incident, however, De León and Manchola seized the contraband along with guns belonging to the Old Station colonists, and arrested DeWitt. Leaving his head firmly attached, they removed him to La Bahía for trial. Apparently Stephen F. Austin's intervention finally quieted the matter.

Not surprisingly, the Mexican government ordered DeWitt to abandon Old Station because of its easy access to smuggled goods. Most colonists returned to Gonzales as resentment, distrust, and hatred increasingly characterized the De León-DeWitt relationship. The government's decision was also influenced by the Fredonian Rebellion, which was initiated by the American empresario Haden Edwards in Nacogdoches in December 1826; but Mexican forces aided by Austin colonists squelched the uprising the following month. Furthermore, unlike De León who established a Catholic church in Guadalupe Victoria and utilized the La Bahía priests until securing his own, DeWitt supplied his colony with neither church nor priest (a Cumberland Presbyterian missionary did occasionally visit), despite the stipulation in his contract to do so.

Indians remained troublesome for La Bahía, Guadalupe Victoria, Gonzales, and San Felipe. De León's reputation as an Indian fighter was widely known and respected. By 1827 he and Austin launched a campaign against the Karankawas and were assisted by the La Bahía garrison and other Mexican federal troops under General Anastacio Bustamante, who was then in Texas to defeat the Fredonian Rebellion. In May the Karankawas were defeated and a peace treaty signed by Bustamante, Martín and Fernando De León, Jacob Betts (for Austin), Green DeWitt, and James Kerr, as well as by Father Miguel Miro in behalf of the

Indians. DeWitt colonists were also able to negotiate a peace with the Tonkawas, but the settlers were still subjected to Comanche raids, which were particularly bad in 1830. Despite DeWitt's prompting, the Mexican government was unable to send troops or establish a garrison at Gonzales because the few available soldiers had to be concentrated at La Bahía and San Antonio, which suffered raids more frequently. As a defense measure the jefe político in San Antonio did send the citizens of Gonzales a cannon, which ironically would be used against Mexican forces in the first battle of the Texas Revolution.

Austin's inspiration and the opportunities afforded by liberal Mexican colonization policy brought two additional settlements to the rich coastal plains of Texas in 1828: the Irish colonies of James Power and James Hewetson at Refugio, and of John McMullen and James McGloin at San Patricio. McMullen and McGloin obtained a grant to settle two hundred Irish Catholic and Mexican families on the Nueces River. They brought the first families—fifty-one people—in October 1829, though they remained at Mission Refugio for about a year before moving on to establish San Patricio (named for their homeland) in 1831. Moderately successful empresarios, McMullen and McGloin would ultimately issue eighty-four land titles. Power and Hewetson (the latter came with Austin to Texas) were given a grant to settle two hundred Irish Catholic and Mexican families between the Lavaca and Guadalupe rivers in 1828; they would eventually issue 200 land titles, though many were to single men rather than to families. In 1829 they successfully petitioned the government to extend their lands from the Guadalupe to the Nueces. Not surprisingly, border disputes and other conflicts occurred between these two Irish colonies and also with De León's.

The dispute with De León resulted when Power and Hewetson petitioned the Mexican authorities to increase their lands again to include acreage once belonging to the abandoned Mission Refugio. De León worked closely through the ayuntamiento of La Bahía to achieve a compromise: the Irish empresarios would get the former mission lands while accepting the Coleto Creek rather than the Guadalupe River as their northeast boundary.

Furthermore, the Irishmen's grant stipulated that they had to respect the rights of La Bahía citizens who were already settled in the area. Notably, this included Carlos de la Garza, who was born at La Bahía in 1807, the son of a Mexican soldier then stationed with the royal Spanish garrison.

De la Garza established a family ranch about 1825 at Carlos Crossing, about twelve miles below Goliad on the San Antonio River in what is now Victoria County. It was located on the old road from Victoria to Refugio. The settlement grew into a village known as Carlos Rancho having its own church and resident priest. In 1834 De la Garza received title in the Power and Hewetson colony for a league of land that included the family ranch, Carlos Crossing, and Carlos Rancho. The population of this village would grow substantially in 1835–1836 as the Tejano[7] residents of Goliad abandoned their town after its capture and subsequent occupation by Americans, especially James W. Fannin's command. Consequently, Carlos Rancho would fall suspect as a nest of spies. Its citizens, loyal Mexicans ever disgruntled by the Americans and their enthusiasm to make Texas independent from Mexico, would play a critical role in Fannin's defeat—especially De la Garza's *Victoriana Guardes*, a unit of some eighty mounted rancheros. Indeed, many Tejano rancheros from the San Patricio, Refugio, and Goliad areas, incensed with their treatment by the Americans in Fannin's command, would serve as independent advance cavalry for Gen. José de Urrea's Mexican army.

In 1829, the year La Bahía town was rechristened as "Goliad," Martín De León received permission to bring in an additional 150 families ("most of them to be Mexican") and to augment his own colony. With the help of the ayuntamiento of Goliad he petitioned the government in 1831 to annul the Power and Hewetson contract so that "those lands thereby remain to be distributed to the inhabitants of Goliad, or for the benefit of the Empresario Martín De León." But this time the government ruled that De León was encroaching, refused to nullify the Power-Hewetson contract, and annulled De León's boundary augmentation.

Good relations did develop between the two colonies nevertheless, a relationship that proved an important alliance during the

Texas Revolution. John J. Linn, who became a liaison between Mexican and Irish colonists and was called "Juan Linn" by Tejanos among whom he was popular, was granted land in the Power and Hewetson colony though he maintained his residence and business in Guadalupe Victoria. And José Miguel Aldrete, De León's son-in-law, became the largest landowner in the Irish colony (present Refugio County). His ranch was not far from the Mission Refugio, where he lived at various times.

Though unsuccessful at expanding his southwestern boundaries into Power and Hewetson territory, De León did manage to extend his colony on the northeast into his older adversary's grant. DeWitt's colony was adversely affected by the Law of April 6, 1830, which prohibited further immigration into Texas from the United States. Austin managed to get the government to exclude DeWitt's settlement from the ruling, but the arrival of new families decreased to a such a trickle that his contract expired unfulfilled on April 15, 1831. Nor was he granted an extension (he ultimately issued titles to 166 families). Since the greater portion of DeWitt's grant was still unoccupied, the vacant lands reverted to the government to dispose of to any empresario it wished.

After much dispute and petitioning, the government ruled in May 1832 to issue grants to Martín De León and another Mexican empresario, Juan Vicente Campos, though they, too, had to respect the rights of previous settlers. Among the titles that De León issued pertaining to these former DeWitt lands was one to his loyal ally and son-in-law, Rafael Manchola. Although De León died in the great cholera epidemic of 1833–1834,[8] between 100 and 200 titles were given to his colonists by July 1835, making him the only empresario besides Austin who completely fulfilled his contract. And, aided by its vital connection with Goliad and La Bahía, Guadalupe Victoria emerged as a leading center of commercial activity, eclipsing Gonzales, Refugio, San Patricio, Carlos Rancho, and even Goliad itself. Despite their adversarial beginnings, however, all of these settlements would soon find themselves allied in the political movement to make Texas a Mexican state independent of Coahuila. But they would become torn once again as this revolution gained the momentum brought largely by Americans to make Texas independent of Mexico altogether. Rechristened as Goliad, the old presidial settlement would again become the crucial focus.

Rafael Manchola had only been recently elected the Texas deputy to the congress of Coahuila y Texas when he had proposed to the government early in 1829 that the name of his village be changed, "in view of the great confusion and the misunderstandings that have arisen...because of the meaningless name of the Presidio La Bahía del Espíritu Santo which is not at all appropriate." Neither mission nor presidio had been located on "the bay" since 1726. He then asked that "this august Congress declare the place a Town with the name of Goliad, which is an anagram made from the surname [Hidalgo] of the heroic giant of our revolution." On February 4, 1829, the government had proclaimed the settlement a villa—a capital town with municipality jurisdiction—and changed its name to Goliad. The momentous events of 1835-36 would insure that the new name would acquire a distinction unique beyond all of Manchola's expectations.

# 3.
# REVOLUTION!

*We have either to fight for our homes or fly and leave them.*
—PHILIP DIMMITT, COLONIST
AND COMMANDER, GOLIAD, 1835

*That the former province and department of Texas is, and of a right ought to be a free, sovereign and independent state.*
—GOLIAD DECLARATION OF INDEPENDENCE, 1835

*We can not rationally anticipate any other result to our Quixotic expedition than total defeat.*
—JOHN SOWERS BROOKS
FANNIN'S COMMAND, GOLIAD, 1836

THE EMERGENCE OF ANTONIO LÓPEZ DE SANTA ANNA as president of Mexico in 1834, and consequently his leadership in a movement to establish the authority of a supreme central government, was the ironic catalyst toward a rebellion in the northern provinces that would ultimately result in revolution and Texas independence. Citizens of Coahuila y Texas grew discontented with the Centralist policies of their new president and claimed an adherence to the Federalist Constitution of 1824, which limited the power of the central government. At the same time Santa Anna was determined to suppress any movements dedicated to maintaining federalism and opposing his presidency.[9]

Santa Anna led the first significant assault against federalism in the spring of 1835 by crushing the city of Zacatecas. He then ordered Gen. Martín Perfecto de Cos, his brother-in-law, to Texas in September to investigate the refusal of citizens at Anahuac to pay duties to the central government. Cos was to proceed to San Antonio and ultimately San Felipe de Austin through Goliad with an army of 500 men, whose purpose was to reinforce Col. Domingo de Ugartechea and chastise the citizens of Texas for their attitude. This plan was well known in Texas, for many citizens had family and business connections with interior Mexico. The influential John J. Linn of Guadalupe Victoria, for example, warned that Cos would land at Copano as early as July 1835.

## THE CAMPAIGN OF 1835

The first moves to suppress rebellious intent in Texas were resisted in ways similar to initial events in the American Revolution— by citizen militia and newly formed committees of safety and correspondence. In July at La Bahía presidio, Col. Nicolás Condelle, who had been sent to secure Goliad and Copano for Cos's upcoming expedition, arrested the alcalde, stripped the town of its arms, pressed citizens into service, and quartered soldiers in their homes. Clashes between the Mexican soldiers and area settlers occurred several times, paralleling the events occurring some sixty miles away at Gonzales.

Various Texas citizens including Philip Dimmitt, John J. Linn, and James Walker Fannin made plans to intercept Cos at Copano or Goliad and so prevent his march to San Antonio, but the Mexican general landed unopposed at Copano about September 20. James Power, empresario of the Power and Hewetson colony and Cos's friend, sought out the general, who cordially informed the empresario of his orders to "repress with strong arm all those who, forgetting their duties to the nation which has adopted them as her children, are pushing forward with a desire to live at their own option without subjection to the laws." Power then warned

Lithograph of President-General Antonio López de Santa Anna from Don Lucas Alaman's *Historia de Mejico* (1852). *Courtesy Benson Latin American Collection, University of Texas at Austin.*

the inland colonies that Cos had arrived and was marching to reinforce the government garrisons at Refugio, Goliad, and San Antonio, and would ultimately arrive at San Felipe de Austin. The landing and transport of munitions, provisions, and supplies were assisted by Condelle's La Bahía garrison, with carts and reluctant laborers impressed into service from among the Refugio colonists and the citizens of Goliad.

Cos left Refugio on October 1 and entered Goliad the next day with an honor guard of thirty, followed soon thereafter by the

Morelos infantry battalion, which numbered more than 400. He dispatched Capt. Manuel Sabriego, a commander of local rancheros, and about twenty-five men to Guadalupe Victoria to seize a cannon and arrest Jóse M. J. Carbajal, De León's well-known son-in-law. Like the incident at Gonzales, the attempt was unsuccessful. Alcalde Plácido Benavides, also a De León son-in-law, led the militia of Victoria against surrendering either the cannon or Carbajal. Meanwhile, the excitement erupting at Gonzales on and before September 29 both deterred Fannin's proposed attack on Cos and accelerated the Mexican general's march to San Antonio. The Texan volunteer companies moving to intercept Cos abandoned that objective and hurried instead to Gonzales, where the first armed clash of the revolution occurred on October 2. Among the defenders at the battle of Gonzales was James Walker Fannin, the captain of the Brazos Guards.

Cos departed from Goliad on October 5 with his honor guard and the Morelos Battalion and marched unmolested toward San Antonio, leaving behind a small detachment of twenty-seven men at La Bahía under Lt. Col. Francisco Sandoval and Capt. Sabriego. The general left another garrison under command of Capt. Nicolás Rodríguez at Fort Lipantitlán, a strategically important fort located to the south on the Nueces River near San Patricio.[10] Sabriego was also charged with guarding Cos's supplies, which had to be left at Goliad because no transportation was available.

Despite the action at Gonzales, not all citizens diverted their attention from Goliad. Linn and Benavides, who had gone to Gonzales to train the volunteers amassing there after the battle, tried to persuade these men to intercept Cos before he reached San Antonio; but finding most unwilling, the two joined a company of about fifty men under Ben Fort Smith and William H. Jack, who set out to liberate Goliad and Copano from Mexican occupation. Another company of about forty men, mostly from the Matagorda area, organized under Capt. George M. Collinsworth, then marched to Guadalupe Victoria, picking up recruits along the way. The force reached Victoria on October 9. There the men ate, rested, and were reinforced by some thirty additional volunteers from Victoria, Goliad, and the surrounding area, including

Silvestre De León, Carbajal, Dimmitt, and Benavides, who had arrived with Linn ahead of Smith's company. Linn sent word to Refugio asking for volunteers; many arrived in time to participate in the attack. On October 9 the company avowed their intention to "take up the line of March for Goliad" by signing the "Compact of Volunteers," a solemn pledge to "give the population of that town protection against military domination . . . [and to] stand firm to the Republican institutions of the Govt. of Mexico and of Coahuila & Texas under the constitution of 1824." Collinsworth's company ultimately numbered some 120 men.

While at Victoria, Dimmitt, a De León colonist, received word from a contact at Goliad that Cos was on his way to San Antonio and had left only a small garrison at the old presidio. Collinsworth marched his company southwestward across the prairie and after dark reached Manahuilla Creek, where they rested and sent a small party under Ira Ingram to scout the town. They were surprised by the appearance of Benjamin R. Milam, who had just escaped from prison in Monterrey and was traveling "to reach my countrymen in Texas." The well-known Milam was welcomed into Collinsworth's company, which resumed its march. Guided by those familiar with the area, the men reached Presidio La Bahía at about 11:00 P.M.; the scouting party was now reunited with the main unit. Before, during, and after the assault the company was additionally reinforced by James Power, Ira J. Westover, and other volunteers from the Refugio area. The Texans took the garrison by surprise and battled for about thirty minutes before capturing the presidio. Casualties were light on both sides. The Texans suffered several wounded but none killed; the Mexican force lost three killed and seven wounded. Sandoval and Sabriego were among the twenty-one prisoners, though almost twenty Mexican soldiers escaped to warn the Copano and Refugio garrisons, which then removed to Fort Lipantitlán. Sandoval also was able to send word to Cos.

Linn, who became quartermaster of the army on October 8, and DeWitt's surveyor James Kerr had remained at Guadalupe Victoria to gather recruits, munitions, and provisions to bring to Goliad, where the two arrived on October 11. Volunteers continued to arrive until a regiment of about 100 men was organized and elected Ben Fort Smith as colonel, Collinsworth as major, and Dimmitt as captain. Gen. Stephen F. Austin soon ordered part of the garrison to join the siege underway at San Antonio de Béxar. Among the companies heading for Béxar were those of Smith and Benavides, while Collinsworth left to recruit men at Matagorda. Those remaining at Goliad elected Dimmitt their leader. Ben Milam escorted Sandoval, Sabriego, and other captured Mexican officers to San Felipe via Gonzales, where Gen. Austin freed Sabriego to return to his family at Goliad. At Linn's urging the remaining Mexican prisoners at La Bahía were released on their own recognizance. Sabriego later escaped to Mexico and returned as a leader of the Badeños, Tejano citizens of La Bahía who did not favor the Texas cause—a group perilously alienated by Dimmitt's successor, James Walker Fannin.

Both Dimmitt and Austin saw the necessity of retaining Goliad as strategically essential to defeating Cos at San Antonio de Béxar. During the time that Dimmitt commanded Goliad—from about October 14, 1835, to about January 14, 1836—Austin and others drew upon his captured stores for supplies, provisions, and teams. Once these were depleted, he called upon or forced area colonists to contribute needed supplies (actions that worsened relations with local Badeños, many of whom fled to the countryside). Dimmitt continued to seek reinforcements. He issued an impassioned appeal "To the inhabitants of Texas residing East of the Guadalupe" on October 21, 1835, warning of "a war of Extermination on the part of the Enimey" and asserting that "we have either to fight for our homes or fly and leave them." That same month he sent Linn, Kerr, and Thomas G. Western to negotiate a treaty of neutrality with menacing Karankawas, the only Indians known to have fought on both sides of the revolution. The treaty was generally successful during Dimmitt's command, but Fannin, his ill-fated successor, was not to be so fortunate. Dimmitt also committed himself to evacuating citizens from the Goliad-Refugio war zone to Victoria, Matagorda, and Texana.

The Goliad commander's attack on the Mexican garrison remaining at Fort Lipantitlán proved to be one of the three most

Portrait alleged to be of James W. Fannin attributed to his cousin, Samuel F. B. Morse. *Courtesy Summerfield G. Roberts Collection, Dallas Historical Society.*

significant events of the 1835 campaign, along with Collinsworth's capture of Goliad itself and the Goliad Declaration of Independence (which would be issued later that year). Although Fort Lipantitlán had served primarily as a customs inspection post and way station for overland trade between Texas and the interior, after the fall of Goliad the fort assumed the much more important role of maintaining the only link in the Mexican government's line between Matamoros and Béxar. Sabriego and his Badeños sustained communication between the fort and Béxar, captured

Texan messages, and kept Cos informed. Lipantitlán also effectively prevented the colonists at nearby San Patricio from openly supporting the cause against Santa Anna. More threatening still (though probably unknown to Dimmitt) was Cos's scheme to use Lipantitlán in an attempt to recapture Goliad.

Understanding the strategic importance of Lipantitlán, Dimmitt proposed to capture the fort, a plan approved by Aldrete, Power, Kerr, and Linn, who remained with the Goliad garrison as elder advisers. Indeed, it was Power who discovered that a Mexican force from Lipantitlán was to recapture Goliad. The Dimmitt expedition against the Mexican post marched out of Goliad on October 21, 1835, under command of Ira Westover, Dimmitt's adjutant and a member of his advisory council. Linn, Power, and Kerr, delegates-elect to the Consultation (which met to debate what course Texas should take against Santa Anna), postponed their trip to San Felipe de Austin to counsel the expedition.

The Texan party of almost forty men, which was augmented to perhaps sixty at Refugio, drew the attention of Capt. Rodríguez at Lipantitlán, who sent out most of his garrison of about eighty to intercept the Texans. Meanwhile, Cos had ordered Rodríguez to launch his attack against Goliad as part of the effort to secure Texas—Santa Anna would soon be leading an army to Béxar, and Gen. José de Urrea would be bringing another force through Goliad in February. Rodríguez's expedition thus served two purposes. The Texans evaded detection by avoiding main roads, however, arrived at Lipantitlán on November 3, and in a surprise attack captured the fort, finding the major portion of the garrison away. The next day Rodríguez, recognizing the situation, returned to Lipantitlán and battled Westover's men but was defeated. The victory rallied Texan morale and enabled San Patricio to elect delegates to the Consultation and support the cause favoring the Constitution of 1824.

Dimmitt continued to plan his garrison's role in driving Cos from San Antonio, though his command became increasingly beset with troubles. Upon returning to Goliad after the Lipantitlán expedition, Westover's force encountered a party that included Dr. James Grant[11] and the Federalist governor of Coahuila y Texas,

Agustín Viesca, recently escaped from a Matamoros prison. Dimmitt, who was now leaning toward independence from Mexico rather than simply supporting the Federalist cause, refused to recognize Viesca's authority, and act which outraged Linn, Kerr, Grant, and local Tejanos still loyal to the Constitution of 1824. Austin was soon beleaguered with letters of protest against Dimmitt's conduct. Fearing that the cooperation of the Federalists of northern Mexico against Santa Anna might be jeopardized, Austin removed Dimmitt from command without a hearing on November 18. The General Council, however, which also rejected Viesca's authority, refused to remove Dimmitt after his men issued a series of resolutions protesting Austin's action.

The Viesca incident occurred while Dimmitt was trying to restore his authority among those in his command eager to join Robert C. Morris's New Orleans Greys, who passed through Goliad en route to join the siege against Cos at Béxar. Faced with a mutinous situation, Dimmitt put Presidio La Bahía and the town of Goliad under martial law briefly until the disorder was quelled. The Greys, now mounted and provisioned from the Goliad stores, proceeded to Béxar on November 19. Still, Dimmitt's men remained eager to join the movement against Cos, an interest not lost on their captain.

Though concerned with Cos, Dimmitt also contemplated an expedition against Matamoros, an idea he originated (despite its usual attribution to James Grant and Francis W. Johnson). Indeed, the assault against Fort Lipantitlán was part of this scheme. Dimmitt was well informed of Mexican plans and movements through trusted Tejano and Irish colonists of the Victoria-Goliad-Refugio-San Patricio area. He had learned that the cooperation of Federalists in northern Mexico against Centralists at Matamoros and Béxar was very likely forthcoming in late November and early December 1835, and even suggested that Gen. Lorenzo de Zavala lead the assault. Though Austin favored the idea of an expedition against Matamoros led by Mexican Federalists of the interior, he was more immediately interested in assaulting Béxar, a concern necessarily shared by Dimmitt. The Matamoros project failed to materialize after Federalist Gen. José Antonio Mexía's defeat at Tampico, and because of the antagonism engendered by Grant and Johnson's attempt to launch their own assault on Matamoros.

Although Austin's army, provisioned by Dimmitt, had held Cos under siege at Béxar since October, an attack had not been made, and it became questionable whether an assault was preferable to abandoning the siege and falling back to the fortifications that La Bahía offered at Goliad before Santa Anna's main army could arrive from Mexico. When Edward Burleson succeeded Austin as general of the army after the latter was sent to the United States by the provisional government, the new commander dispatched his adjutant and inspector general, Col. James Bowie, to Presidio La Bahía to "superintend the strengthening of the fortifications." Bowie arrived at Goliad about November 29, found Dimmitt's expedition to Béxar now underway, and apparently joined it. About December 6 Dimmitt, probably Bowie, and a contingent of the Goliad garrison including De León son-in-law José Miguel Aldrete, proceeded to Béxar. (Plácido Benavides, Silvestre De Leon, and a company of Victoria rancheros were already there, fighting in Francis W. Johnson's command.) They participated in the final assault that had been launched by Ben Milam the morning of December 5. Cos's defeat delivered Béxar to the Texans, who already controlled Goliad and Copano, the keys to South Texas.

Dimmitt's party, probably with Bowie, returned to Goliad about December 14, its commander now convinced of the necessity of Texas independence from Mexico, since Mexía's action at Tampico failed to stir up a Federalist insurrection against Santa Anna in the eastern states of Mexico. Dimmitt designed what has been called the first Texas flag of independence, decorated with a bloody arm holding a bloody sword on a white field, and raised it on December 20 to commemorate the declaration that he and Ira Ingram framed, proclaiming Texas "a free, sovereign and independent State," promising "equal, impartial, and indiscriminate protection to all." Ninety-two signers ratified the document, including many Irish colonists and, significantly, colonists of Mexican descent, notably José Miguel Aldrete and José M. J. Carbajal. The

Goliad Declaration of Independence was printed and widely distributed. It preceded the March 2, 1836, declaration issued by the Convention at Washington-on-the-Brazos by seventy-two days. The General Council, however, fearing loss of cooperation with Federalists in northern Mexico, criticized the Goliad document as premature and filed the original copy without further action.

In early January 1836 Johnson and Grant's controversial expedition against Matamoros, already having depleted the stores at Béxar, passed through Goliad en route to San Patricio. Grant commandeered Dimmitt's supplies and horses, and ordered the Goliad flag of independence to be lowered, fearing it would alienate Mexican Federalists. Dimmitt consented only to avoid armed confrontation between their two forces. With the provisional government split over the situation and offering no relief, Dimmitt resigned his command in protest. Only a personal appearance at Goliad by Sam Houston quieted the post—but even he was unable to stop Johnson and Grant's expedition, which he criticized as folly. Sadly, despite crucial Texan victories at Copano, Goliad, Lipantitlán, San Patricio, and Béxar, Texan forces and the provisional government remained divided as to purpose, Béxar and Goliad suffered weakened conditions, and provisions became critically scarce, all at a crucial time foreshadowing the imminent arrival of the Centralist army under Santa Anna.

## THE CAMPAIGN OF 1836

By early 1836 the Texans[12] had available a considerable number of men to deploy against the advancing Mexican army. Most were volunteers; some were regular troops. Col. James Walker Fannin landed at Copano on February 2 with about 200 men, including William Ward's Georgia Battalion, Burr H. Duval's Kentucky Mustangs, and Luis Guerra's Mexican artillery company (later discharged). Six small companies, amounting to another 200 men, awaited Fannin at Refugio; sixty more volunteers were at San Patricio under Francis W. Johnson and James Grant, still anxious to attack Matamoros. Another eighty, including Capt. John (Jack) Shackelford's Alabama company of Red Rovers, were encamped on the Lavaca River awaiting Fannin's call. Two strong companies, 100 men, recruited by Capt. Amasa Turner in New Orleans and Velasco, were at the mouth of the Brazos under orders to report to Fannin at Copano; and Edwin Morehouse's New York Battalion had, on January 20, renewed its voyage to Texas from Nassau. This force, 190 strong, had sailed from New York on November 21, 1835, on the brig *Mattawamkeag* but had been detained in the Bahamas for two months on charges of piracy. William P. Miller, commissioned in December 1835 as a major of the Texas Cavalry, was recruiting his Nashville Battalion in Tennessee. This force of of seventy-five men would sail from New Orleans aboard the schooner *William and Frances* for Copano in early March hoping to join Fannin. Francis W. Thorton, with a small company of regulars, occupied the old presidio at Goliad; and James C. Neill had 150 men at San Antonio to defend the Alamo and the town of Béxar. As for civilian populations in the war zone, Victoria and Refugio area colonists largely supported the Texas cause, while those of Béxar, San Patricio, and Goliad were bitterly divided, the latter two remaining predominantly pro-Mexican.

Fannin went to Copano as agent of the provisional government to organize yet another Matamoros expedition—designed to aid Mexican Federalists against Santa Anna's Centralists—after Francis W. Johnson declined the offer following a disagreement with the General Council. With Sam Houston on self-appointed furlough (a move designed to check the dissent generated against him for his opposition to a Matamoros campaign), Fannin was the senior Texas officer in the field. On February 4 and 5, he marched the companies he had with him at Copano to the Texan camp at Refugio as a step toward the proposed Matamoros expedition, only to learn, on February 7 through Capt. Plácido Benavides of the De León Colony, that Santa Anna's threatened movement to overwhelm Texas and suppress the rebellion was already under way. Benavides had obtained crucial information from the alcalde of Matamoros, warning that the Mexican president planned to attack Béxar and Goliad simultaneously with two separate forces and that a trap awaited any Texans attacking Matamoros, where the Mexican army was then gathering.

Fannin dispatched William G. Cooke with two companies to reinforce San Patricio and removed his own headquarters to Presidio La Bahía at Goliad, leaving Amon B. King with his small garrison at Refugio and John Chenoweth with a few mounted men to guard Copano, the crucial port for Refugio, Goliad, and San Antonio. After Fannin successfully relocated at Goliad, Shackelford and his Alabama Red Rovers joined him on February 12. Fannin ultimately reorganized his diverse Goliad command into a single regiment consisting of the Georgia Battalion and the Lafayette Battalion.

Organized by William Ward in Macon, Georgia, following a town meeting in November 1835, the "Georgia Battalion of Permanent Volunteers" holds a special place in the Texas saga. Ward enlisted about 120 men from Macon, Milledgeville, Savannah, and Columbus, Georgia (Fannin's home state) and armed, supplied, and transported them to Texas at personal expense and with the aid of the State of Georgia arsenal. The battalion passed through Knoxville, Georgia, where Johanna Troutman—called the "Betsy Ross of Texas"— presented them with her "Flag of the Lone Star." Handsewn of white silk embroidered with a single blue five-pointed star, the banner bore the mottoes "Liberty or Death" (some accounts have it as "Texas and Liberty") and "Ubi Libertas Habitat, Ibi Nostra Patria Est" ("Where Liberty Dwells, There Is Our Country").[13] Ward continued recruiting volunteers along the way to New Orleans until the battalion numbered about 220 men. On December 20, 1835, the men landed at Velasco, Texas, where Ward presented their services to Fannin on December 23. It was the Troutman flag that Fannin raised over Presidio La Bahía on March 8, 1836, upon hearing that the Convention had declared Texas independent on March 2. The imagery of the battalion's "Lone Star" flag proved a timeless and compelling emblem among the Texans.

Meantime, disaster had struck at the mouth of the Brazos. The schooner *Tamaulipas*, carrying Turner's two companies and the

Texas army's whole supply of munitions, clothing, and shoes—badly needed by Fannin's volunteers—was wrecked on February 5 on the Brazos sand bar. Turner and his men were now employed in salvaging the cargo. Fannin learned at the same time that New Orleans underwriters had refused to insure Texas-bound cargoes consigned via Aransas Pass, thereby effectively terminating all plans for using Copano as a base. Provisions, arms, and munitions now had to be consigned via Pass Cavallo and the Matagorda ports (Dimmitt's Landing, Cox's Point, Linnville) and hauled overland from there.

Withdrawal to Goliad was Fannin's own idea, and it proved to be a tragic mistake. He gave as his reason for fortifying Goliad his "conviction of its importance, as being advantageously located for a depot of reinforcements, clothing, provisions and military stores. It commands the sea coast, particularly Aransas and Matagorda Bays—and consequently the only convenient landings for vessels of any tonnage." Fannin, trained at the United States Military Academy at West Point, understood Goliad's strategic importance in relation to Béxar. Santa Anna knew this, too. But for the Texas cause, Goliad could remain pivotal only as long as Texans held Béxar, and it was questionable how effectively Fannin could command the Aransas Bay area some forty miles away against Santa Anna's advance. The village of Guadalupe Victoria actually offered a more defensible and friendly place from which to command Matagorda Bay—where the supplies were—but Goliad offered better housing facilities and was a shorter distance from Refugio, where Fannin's command had been stationed without tents and with little shelter.

When Fannin withdrew to Goliad on February 12, Santa Anna's force was already on the march, with light cavalry and local Tejano rancheros, particularly from the Refugio and Goliad areas, serving as advance units gathering intelligence—an advantage not lost on the Goliad commander. As early as February 7 Fannin wrote, "It is useless to controvert the fact that our true strength and geographical situation are well known to Santa Anna." By contrast, Fannin had no mounted troops to use for scouting the Mexican advance, and remained generally ignorant of their movements. Santa Anna's main army of some 6,000 men was moving through Laredo toward Béxar, where his advance column arrived on February 23. Meanwhile, his right wing, more than 1,000 strong and led by the talented and energetic Gen. José de Urrea, left encampment at Matamoros and began marching toward San Patricio on February 13, en route ultimately to Goliad, Victoria, and Brazoria, to command access to the Gulf of Mexico.

Urrea's first objective was the raiding party under Johnson and Grant, who had left San Patricio for Tamaulipas, leaving behind three cannon and ammunition. Learning of this, Fannin dispatched a party to bring the artillery to Goliad. In the meantime, William Barret Travis, now sharing a divided command at Béxar, sent James Butler Bonham, Fannin's long-time friend, to confer with the army's "Acting Commander-in-Chief" (in Houston's absence) at Goliad. As a result Fannin toyed with the idea of moving his headquarters to Béxar or at least reinforcing the garrison that occupied the Alamo, but nothing was done. Fannin continued to fortify and rebuild the old presidio at Goliad, which he renamed Fort Defiance. This work was still unfinished when Travis's call for help reached Goliad on February 25.

Fannin planned to leave the next day with 320 volunteers and four pieces of artillery to join Travis at the Alamo. He also intended to call his units scattered in Copano and Refugio back to Goliad. But Fannin's march to relieve Travis ended on the banks of the San Antonio River only two miles from Fort Defiance—an ironic foretaste of the tragedy yet to come. Wagons broke down, oxen strayed, provisions were scarce, and the volunteers, anxious for a fight, all insisted on going along; only Ira Westover's regulars agreed to stay at Goliad. (Maintaining discipline could be problematic in the Texas army given the proud, if not rebellious, democratic spirit among its volunteers). "Col. Fannin was truly a brave and good soldier but too free and good natured for a commander," wrote Capt. Benjamin H. Hughes of the Georgia Battalion, who criticized Fannin for lacking "the necessary austerity for a commander to enforce disiplin." The men behaved as if "in a general confused mob." Many were barefooted and poorly clothed, yet faced a well-provisioned and trained enemy of superi-or numbers. Fannin's aide-de-camp, John Sowers Brooks, wrote prophetically, "we can not rationally anticipate any other result to our Quixotic expedition than total defeat."

Despite this desperate supply situation, Fannin returned to Goliad rather than move toward provisions at the Matagorda ports some sixty miles away for fear of exposing these supplies and because the provisional government, not perceiving the actual field situation, had ordered him not to retreat from Goliad. Fannin, who tragically was becoming increasingly doubtful him-self of his own ability to command, continued fortifying the old presidio and awaiting orders from the government. The two-day attempt to relieve Béxar cost him precious time and popularity. It also caused bitter resentment among many of his men, especially the New Orleans Greys—now called the San Antonio Greys—who became increasingly critical of Fannin's command capabilities. Furthermore, he incurred ill feelings through his involvement in a quarrel within the provisional government between the General Council and Governor Henry Smith over the Matamoros expedi-tion, an involvement that also strained his relationship with his second in command, William Ward.

Meanwhile at San Patricio, Johnson and Grant were still deter-mined to carry out their expedition against Matamoros, and Urrea was eager to subdue them. Taking advantage of a freezing-cold and rainy norther, and Capt. Sabriego's reconnaissance, the Mexican army surprised Johnson's thirty-four men at San Patricio at three o'clock in the morning, February 27; all were killed or cap-tured except Johnson and four others who escaped. Then on March 2 at Agua Dulce Creek, twenty-six miles below San Patricio, Urrea surprised Grant's party, which had been capturing horses. Grant and thirteen of his men were killed, six captured, and six escaped, including Plácido Benavides, who reported the event to Fannin at Goliad.

With Travis under siege at the Alamo, and with Copano ren-dered useless by Urrea's advance, Fannin's small force could serve no good purpose by staying at Goliad, as Fannin himself well knew. He wrote Acting Governor James W. Robinson on February

22, "I learn from several sources, that as soon as Béxar is retaken, they next march here, and thus complete their chain of communication to the Interior and Gulf. I am resolved to await your orders, let the consequence be what it may. But I say to you, candidly . . . that unless the people of Texas, forthwith, turn out in mass . . . those *now* in the field will be sacrificed . . . if we are not to be sustained in a proper manner, and in good time, receive orders to fall back to the Provisions, and on the Colonies, and *let us all go together*. . . . I have orders from you *not* to make a *retrograde movement*, but to await orders and reinforcements. If a large [enemy] force gets here, and in possession of the provisions and stores of Matagorda Bay, *being all now in Texas*, it will be a desperate game for us all."

Governor Robinson's order "not to make a retrograde movement" was coupled with orders "to hold your position at Copano, and if possible, at San Patricio." Fannin had attempted neither, wanting to maintain an option in the event of an attack by a superior force. He sought only to pass on to higher authority the responsibility for an order he knew would be unpopular with his men, who, having toiled resentfully to fortify the old Goliad presidio, were now eager to confront the Mexican army—certainly not to retreat. Thus, rebuilding the fort immobilized the force and compelled it to a defense.

Fannin imagined that his letter to Robinson (which carried Benavides's warning of February 7 that Santa Anna's army was en route) had aroused Texas colonists and that they would hurry to Goliad as they had hurried to Gonzales in 1835. But it was Travis's ringing calls from the Alamo, and not Fannin's letter, that brought the colonists into the field in 1836. Indeed, by late February Fannin had lost confidence in the Texas colonists; their refusal to reinforce his army angered him. It does not seem to have occurred to him that many area colonists already in service under Dimmitt, Linn, and others were gathering elsewhere, sensing the indefensibility of Goliad in the wake of Urrea's advance. Frustrating him further, the members of the Convention of 1836, which was organizing the *ad interim* government for the newly declared Republic of Texas, had no appreciation of the danger and took no measures to meet the coming emergency. Even as late as March 5 the Convention supposed (wrongly) that Fannin had united with Travis, that other reinforcements had joined them in San Antonio, and that the Alamo was safe.

Fannin thought Fort Defiance was ready to withstand a siege by March 1, though ammunition was not too plentiful and provisions were dangerously scarce. He sent a detail to Cox's Point and Dimmitt's Landing on Matagorda Bay to obtain these needed supplies, but the wagons did not return to Goliad until March 10 and 11. Meanwhile, numerous companies of volunteers thought to be en route to join Fannin's command (such as Morehouse's New York Battalion and Miller's Nashville Battalion), were detained and remained scattered at various places. Acting Governor Robinson wrote Fannin on March 6 to "use your own discretion to remain where you are or to retreet as you may think best for the safety of the brave Volunteers Under your command." Ironically, Travis's letter of March 3 (his final plea for reinforcements) reached the Convention only after the Alamo had fallen on March 6. After reading this letter and without realizing the Alamo's fate, Sam Houston, now commander-in-chief of the military forces of the Republic, ordered Neill at Gonzales and Fannin at Goliad to undertake joint action to aid Travis. Fannin received this order on March 12. The next day he was preparing to start for Cibolo Creek with 300 men to meet Houston, when a cry for help came from Capt. Amon B. King, whom he had sent with his available carts and teams and some thirty men to Refugio on March 11 to remove some colonists still stranded there.

Despite a warning from Houston in January against sending out small parties when the Mexican army was so near, Fannin had sent out at least two. The first was on March 10 under William C. Francis of Shackelford's company, which was to evict a suspected "nest of spies" at nearby Carlos Rancho. These people included those disaffected Goliad citizens, the Badeños, who did not favor independence from Mexico and who had been angered particularly at Fannin's arrogant attitude toward them. About six Tejano residents were captured and made prisoners, only later to find themselves in the fury of the battle of Coleto. The second was

King's mission, which was particularly shortsighted on Fannin's part, since King was sent directly into Urrea's known path with enough men to attract attention but too few to repel attack by the Mexican army. This turned out to be the initial significant misjudgment that ended in catastrophe for Fannin's command.

Fannin's march to join Neill awaited King's return. On March 12 while collecting the scattered colonists, King, despite his orders to return to Goliad immediately, decided to search out and punish some marauding bands of Mexicans and Karankawan Indians who had been plundering the deserted countryside. In so doing he blundered upon Capt. Carlos de la Garza's *Victoriana Guardes* serving as Urrea's advance cavalry. King managed to gather the colonists and retreat with them into old Mission Refugio, which was soon surrounded by De la Garza's rancheros and those of Capt. Guadalupe de los Santos, and reportedly, some forty Karankawas. Urrea also sent a picket of regulars under Capt. Rafael Pretalia, bringing Mexican forces to probably about 200. Still, King got word to Fannin for help.

The Goliad commander received King's plea at 1:00 A.M. on March 13 and ordered his second officer, William Ward, and the Georgia Battalion to King's relief. Fannin's orders to Ward, like his aborted march on February 25 to relieve Travis and his orders to King, were basically issued on impulse, without any real consideration of the military problems involved. Sending Ward's detachment, which like most of the Goliad garrison was wholly inexperienced, to Refugio meant placing one-third of the Goliad garrison—more men that Travis had had in the Alamo—without provisions, transport, or reserve ammunition, and without proper support, directly in the path of Urrea's advancing main army.

Ward left Goliad at 3:00 A.M. on March 13, force-marched twenty-seven miles across rain-soaked prairie, and relieved the besieged King at about three that afternoon. After his initial skirmish Ward decided to rest his men overnight before returning to Fort Defiance. Meanwhile, Santa Anna was sending reinforcements to Urrea from Béxar, and Urrea was advancing toward Refugio, having been informed of Ward's movements through ranchero scouts. Leaving the main army under Col. Francisco

Garay to follow, Urrea marched from the Aransas River with 180 infantry, 100 cavalry, and an artillery piece. Had Ward shown equal energy, and had he and King not argued, they might have arrived safely at Goliad at dawn the following day.

Instead of returning to Goliad, however, Ward and his men, like King's, were eager for a fight, and they found one early the next day, March 14. Quarreling with Ward, King refused to return to Goliad until he had punished local rancheros. His party of twenty-eight men then ambushed and killed eight local Tejanos assumed to be spies. Indeed, one of them had been in Luis Guerra's Mexican artillery company, formerly of Fannin's command, and was found with communications to Urrea written while he had been at Fort Defiance. (The Mexican general skillfully utilized Tejanos suspicious of, or resentful to, the Texas cause.) Meanwhile, Ward sent a force under his second in command, Dr. Warren Jordan Mitchell, on a reconnoitering mission. As Urrea's main army of some 1,500 men approached, Mitchell's detachment returned to the protection offered by the old Refugio mission.

Suffering heavy losses conservatively estimated at 100 dead and fifty wounded, excluding ranchero casualties, Urrea launched several vigorous assaults on Ward's position, all of which the Texans repulsed with minor casualties. King's detachment, returning in mid-afternoon by nearby Mission River, stumbled upon the rear of Urrea's army and was at once attacked. King took a position in some woods on the river's bank and resisted all efforts by Col. Gabriel Núñez's cavalry and Col. Francisco Garay's infantry to dislodge him, valiantly inflicting punishing losses on his assailants until darkness ended the fight. Having exhausted most of their limited ammunition and provisions, both King and Ward tried to escape. Captured dispatches led Urrea to suppose that the Texans would retreat toward Goliad; but Ward's men left the mission that night on the Copano road and, hiding among a herd of cattle, escaped. King crossed the Mission River where it was not fordable, wetting his little remaining gunpowder. When overtaken the next day by De la Garza's rancheros, he was unable to resist. He and his men were returned to the old Refugio mission. In obedience to Santa Anna's governmental decree of December 30, 1835, which commanded death to all armed foreigners in rebellion, most of King's men were shot on March 16. Col. Juan José Holsinger of the Mexican army spared and liberated eight of the men, six of whom were Refugio colonists, including Lewis T. Ayers. The bodies were left unburied on the prairie.

Ward and his command retreated in the riverbottom swamps toward Guadalupe Victoria, where he logically assumed Fannin now would be, since the Goliad commander had ordered him to rendezvous there in the event that his retreat to Goliad was cut off. Urrea left his wounded and a detachment at the Refugio mission under command of Col. Rafael de la Vara, charged also with guarding Copano. Then Urrea dispatched cavalry units and local rancheros to pursue Ward's men. The seasoned Mexican general then proceeded with about 900 soldiers toward Goliad, continuing to reap the harvest of Texan mistakes.

# 4.
# THE GOLIAD MASSACRE

*I fear La Bahia (Goliad) is in siege.*
—SAM HOUSTON, COMMANDER-IN-CHIEF
GONZALES, 1836

*As we passed the door an officer told me we were all to be shot.*
—ANDREW BOYLE, FANNIN'S COMMAND, 1836

*Don't take on so, boys! If we have to die, let's die like brave men!*
—ROBERT FENNER, FANNIN'S COMMAND, 1836

*This day, Palm Sunday, March 27, has been to me a season of most heartfelt sorrow.*
—UNIDENTIFIED MEXICAN OFFICER, 1836

GEN. HOUSTON ARRIVED AT GONZALES ON MARCH 11—the same day Col. Fannin had dispatched Amon King to Refugio—and learned that the Alamo had fallen. He hurried Capt. Francis J. Dusanque to Goliad with these tidings and ordered Fannin to fall back to Guadalupe Victoria "as soon as practicable . . . with your command, and such artillery as can be brought with expedition. The remainder will be sunk in the river." Houston further ordered

Fannin to blow up Fort Defiance, defend and help evacuate Victoria, and forward one-third of his effective force to Gonzales.

Fannin received this order either on March 13 or 14; the day is a matter of considerable historical dispute, since he has been charged with disobeying Houston's command by dispatching Ward and the Georgia Battalion to Refugio to relieve King, then remaining at Goliad to await Ward's return. Houston's order to retreat to Victoria "as soon as practicable" gave Fannin some discretion, however. The more significant question is not why Fannin lingered after March 14, but why he dallied after February 25, when he learned that Santa Anna was at Béxar. Regardless, Houston himself expressed little confidence in Fannin in a letter to James Collinsworth on March 13: "I would not rely on any co-operation from him. . . . The projected expedition to Matamoros, under the agency of the council has already cost us 237 lives; and where the effects are to end, none can foresee. . . . I fear La Bahía (Goliad) is in siege."

## THE BATTLE OF COLETO

Ironically for Fannin, he now had his long-awaited order to retreat but had neither the means to perform it effectively nor an account of his dispatched personnel's whereabouts. Nearly all his carts and teams were with King at Refugio and a third of his garrison under Ward had marched to King's rescue. Meanwhile, at Guadalupe Victoria, a small company of Texans under Capt. Sam A. White was assembling carts and teams that had been gathered primarily from local residents by John J. Linn, alcalde of Victoria and quartermaster of the army. By so doing, Linn deprived his own citizens of a means of escape, though he directed them to Cox's Point. The settlers of Guadalupe Victoria, particularly the De León family, supported the cause against Santa Anna and therefore were legitimately concerned about their treatment by Urrea's approaching Mexican army.

A swift retreat to Victoria was in Fannin's best interest not only because the Guadalupe River made for a more defensible line but because the citizens of Victoria, unlike those of Goliad, were friendly. Also, the village afforded some provisions, and needed reinforcements were already there or nearby. In addition to White's company, Albert C. Horton was near Victoria with more than forty men, many of them mounted. Philip Dimmitt, the former Goliad commander, recruited a company of twenty-one men there as well, though Houston called them to Gonzales; and Morehouse's New York Battalion was reorganizing on Matagorda Bay. Other reinforcements were also in the area, including as Miller's Nashville Battalion, which was off Aransas Pass heading for Copano. Furthermore, the critical supply stores were nearby at Dimmitt's Landing, Cox's Point, and Linnville.

On March 14, while Ward and King were fighting the battle of Refugio, Fannin dispatched successive couriers to them and to Horton and White at Victoria. The expert mounted rancheros of Carlos de la Garza and others captured all of these couriers, whose messages supplied Urrea with exact knowledge of Fannin's situation, strength, and intentions. Fannin, by contrast, having no mounted men and watched on all sides by Mexican cavalry and rancheros, was virtually blind.

Horton (himself a Texas colonist born in Georgia) and thirty-one mounted men escorted the precious teams and carts from Victoria and joined Fannin late on March 14. These were the last reinforcements the Goliad commander received; the garrison now totaled some 330 men, excluding King's and Ward's commands and various unattached supernumeraries. Prudence dictated that Fannin retreat quickly to Victoria. This was what Ward expected him to do, and having first eluded Urrea after the battle of Refugio by marching toward Copano, Ward left the Copano road at Melon Creek and marched across country toward Victoria, where he believed Fannin would be. Fannin, however, spent March 15 and 16 "in vain anticipation of Ward's return," though he did plan for the retreat by selecting nine pieces of artillery to take with him and burying seven others. At 4:00 P.M. on March 17 he learned of King and Ward's defeat through Hugh McDonald Frazer of the Refugio militia, who had volunteered to investigate.

Yet the overly confident commander of Fort Defiance defied prudence. Instead of retreating hastily to Victoria, Fannin spent

March 18 taking "the necessary measures for a retreat in accordance with the resolution of the officers in council last evening." He and his men had no intention of making a hurried retreat, nor any apparent concern for their situation. The men were still ready for a fight, and most did not esteem the prowess of their enemy—a perilously shortsighted attitude their colonel shared, as regimental surgeon Dr. J. H. Barnard commented in his journal: "His former experience in fighting Mexicans had led him to entertain a great contempt for them as soldiers, and led him to neglect to take such precautionary measures as were requisite, from their great numerical superiority."

The wary Urrea, knowing Fannin's intentions, dispatched cavalry units and rancheros to hold the Texans at Goliad, as he had done with Ward at Refugio, and was busy bringing up the remainder of his army to lay siege to Fort Defiance. He also was expecting daily the arrival of reinforcements from Béxar; Santa Anna had sent Col. Juan Morales's Jiménez and San Luis battalions, some 500 veterans of the Alamo assault, to join Urrea's campaign. These men occupied their assigned position on Manahuilla Creek about three miles north of Goliad on March 17; Urrea reached the San Antonio River the same day and joined the troops of Morales the next. Gen. Urrea's army now totaled at least 1,400 men, excluding the 200 rancheros.

Horton had discovered the Morales battalions during a scouting mission on March 17, at which time a council among Fannin and his officers determined to retreat the next morning. At that seemingly opportune time, however, Urrea's advance cavalry appeared, and Horton, sent to chase them, tired his horses. Fannin, mistaking these advance units for the whole of Urrea's army, assumed Fort Defiance would soon be put under siege and so kept the garrison on alert. He ordered the buried cannon dug up and remounted, and the village of La Bahía burned. During this delay the oxen, which were to be hitched to the carts made ready for the removal to Victoria, were left all day without being fed. No retreat was attempted even that night, a delay based on Horton's seeing Mexican troops at the San Antonio River crossing and his concern that the night was too dark to keep to the road.

"We were by no means disposed to run," recorded Dr. Barnard. "We confidently counted on our ability to take ourselves and all our baggage, etc., in safety to Victoria."

At last the retreat was started, but only by 9:00 A.M. the next morning, March 19, under a heavy fog and much confusion. Provisions so painfully accumulated were burned; rations for the march were not saved. The unearthed cannon were spiked. Fannin insisted on taking nine cumbersome brass cannon and about 1,000 muskets, though he neglected to take enough water and food for more than a few meals. The carts were heavily loaded, the hungry oxen unruly. Progress was slow. Horton's cavalry was dispatched to occupy a fording position across the San Antonio River and then to scout for signs of the Mexican army. Urrea, expecting to lay siege to the fort, was unaware of their departure until 11:00 A.M. But the Texans forfeited about an hour of this precious lead time while crossing the San Antonio River—a cart broke down and the largest cannon fell into the river and had to be fished out. Another valuable hour was lost when Fannin ordered the oxen detached for grazing after the column had proceeded about a mile past Manahuilla Creek. Officers John Shackelford, Burr H. Duval, and Ira Westover protested this stop, arguing the column should not rest until reaching the protection of the Coleto Creek timber. Shackelford particularly noted his commander's contempt for the competence of the Mexican army and his disbelief that Urrea would dare follow them—an assumption reflected among Fannin's men.

Urrea had quickly left Goliad without his artillery and the full complement of his force in order to narrow Fannin's two-hour lead. Mexican sources indicate that he set out with 80 cavalry and 360 infantry. He discovered through his mounted scouts the location of Fannin's column and that the rebel force was considerably smaller than supposed, which prompted him to return 100 infantrymen to Goliad to help secure Presidio La Bahía and escort the artillery ordered to join him as soon as possible. Although Horton's cavalry served as advance guards, Fannin's unalert rear guard failed to detect the Mexican cavalry stalking the column. Meanwhile, the Texans had scarcely resumed march after resting the oxen than another cart broke down; its contents had to be transferred to another wagon. Fannin then sent Horton to scout the Coleto Creek timber, now in sight. Suddenly, the Mexican cavalry surprised them from behind. Upon overtaking the lumbering Texan position at about 1:30 P.M., the Mexican commander ordered his cavalry to halt Fannin's advance toward the protective woods. Fannin set up a skirmish line with artillery while the column attempted to reach the Coleto about two miles distant.

Perceiving the danger, Fannin formed his men into a moving square formation and continued toward the closer timber of Perdido Creek less than a mile away, when overtaken by Mexican cavalry. Caught in a valley some six feet below its surroundings, the Texans still tried to get to the more defensible higher ground about four to five hundred yards distant, but their ammunition cart broke down. While Fannin called a council to determine the feasibility of taking what ammunition they could and reaching the woods, Urrea, seeing his advantage, began his attack. With little water, and situated in an open prairie covered with high grass concealing their enemy situated on higher ground, Fannin's men made ready their defense. Their hollow square was three-ranks deep, each man receiving three to four muskets and many having bayonets, rifles, and pistols. The San Antonio Greys and the Red Rovers formed the front line, Burr H. Duval's Mustangs and others including Hugh Frazer's Refugio militia formed the rear, with the left flank defended by Ira Westover's regulars, and the right by the Mobile Greys.[14] The artillery was placed in the corners (except when moved as needed), and Fannin assumed a command position in the rear of the right flank. In addition, an outpost of sharpshooters formed around Abel Morgan's hospital wagon, which became immobilized earlier when an ox was hit by Mexican fire.

Soon after Urrea's cavalry managed to stop Fannin's retreat, the Mexican general amassed his troops and attacked the square. The rifle companies under Col. Juan Morales assaulted the left; the grenadiers and the first regiment of San Luis Battalion charged the right under Urrea's direct supervision; and the Jiménez Battalion under Col. Mariano Salas attacked the front, while Col. Gabriel Núñez's cavalry charged the rear. There is much discrepancy among different sources regarding the numbers of men involved on March 19. Fannin defended his position with between 300 and 400 men. Urrea wrote that he had 80 cavalry and 260 infantry at the time the Texans were overtaken, a figure confirmed by Lt. Col. José Enrique de la Peña, who also stressed that most of the Mexican troops were the Alamo veterans of Col. Morales. Many Texan sources give unrealistically high numbers in Urrea's pursuit force. Clearly, the Mexican general set out with only a small array of veteran troops—probably 300 to 500 men—to ensure catching Fannin, and left orders for a larger force, including artillery, to follow and aid in battling the Texans once engaged by the pursuit troops. Fannin continuously overestimated the true strength of both Urrea's advance forces at Goliad and the pursuit force at the Coleto, became convinced that he was outnumbered regardless of the actuality, and remained on the defensive.

The battle of Coleto[15] lasted until after sunset. The Texans made effective use of their bayonets, multiple muskets, and nine cannon. Despite horrendous fighting and their lack of experience, their square remained unbroken. Survivor accounts describe bullets as "singing like mad hornets" about them, the battle scene as "dreadful to behold. Killed and maimed men and horses were strewn over the plain, the wounded were rending the air with their distressing moans, while a great number of horses without riders were rushing to and fro back upon the enemy's lines increasing the confusion." The terrified Tejano prisoners, taken on the March 10 raid on Carlos Rancho, dug foxholes for refuge during the battle. "I for one, however, didn't blame them," survivor John Duval recorded, "and besides, to tell the truth...I had a great inclination to 'hole up' myself and draw it in after me." Dr. Barnard recorded that seven of his comrades had been killed, sixty wounded (forty severely), Fannin among them.

The Mexican general was impressed with both the "withering fire of the enemy," and their ability to repulse his three charges— "Though our soldiers showed resolution, the enemy was likewise unflinching." He also esteemed Fannin for being "a gentleman and a man of courage." Likewise did the Mexican soldiers fight with ardor, tenacity, and valor. Urrea himself abandoned his general's post and led both infantry and cavalry charges. His casualties were heavy, perhaps some fifty killed and 140 wounded, but accounts vary widely. Ironically, Urrea retired because of ammunition depletion: "I was forced to retire—not without indignation." Yet, Fannin did not recognize or utilize this opportunity—"The enemy seemed unaware of this, for he did not take advantage of a situation that was invaluable to him," De la Peña recorded. At evening Urrea positioned snipers in the tall grass around the square, inflicting additional casualties before Texan sharpshooters were able to quell these attacks by firing at the flashes illuminating the darkness. Ultimately, the Texans suffered ten deaths during the March 19 battle.

Fannin's men anxiously awaited Horton's company with hoped-for reinforcements from Guadalupe Victoria. But Horton, unable to return through enemy lines, and having found Victoria deserted—Linn, White, and Dimmitt had already departed as Houston had ordered—continued on to Gonzales. Ironically, Ward's evasive Georgia Battalion was close enough to hear the Coleto gunfire, but was exhausted and hungry. Urrea knew from captured couriers that Ward and Fannin would try to rendezvous at Victoria, so with the aid of De la Garza's *Victoriana Guardes*, kept the Georgia Battalion isolated in the Guadalupe riverbottom until they surrendered. At the Coleto battlefield, Urrea posted detachments at three points around the square to prevent escape and kept the Texans on stiff watch throughout the night with false bugle calls.

Fannin's position became critical during the night as the lack of food and water and inability to light fires made treating the wounded impossible. Their suffering was made even more unbearable by a cold and rainy norther, and their cries demoralized everyone. The lack of water, which was required to cool and clean the cannon during fire, also guaranteed the artillery to be ineffective at best the next day, especially considering that the artillerists had sustained a high number of casualties. Furthermore, ammunition was low. A council among Fannin and his officers weighing these facts concluded that they could not sustain another day's battle. Yet, the much-debated proposition to escape to the Perdido or Coleto Creek timber under dark and before Urrea received reinforcements was rejected—the men unanimously voted not to abandon the many wounded, as all had a friend or relative among them. They therefore began digging trenches and erecting barricades of carts and dead animals in preparation for the next day's fight. By the time this was completed, the Mexican position had been reinforced with munitions, fresh troops, and two artillery pieces from Goliad. His army now numbering between 700 and 1,000 men, Urrea placed his artillery on the slopes overlooking the Texas position and grouped for battle at 6:15 A.M., March 20.

The Mexican artillery fired one and possibly two rounds, convincing Fannin that making another stand would be futile. Another consultation among his officers produced the decision—despite protests from the San Antonio Greys and Mobile Greys—to seek honorable terms of surrender for the sake of the wounded, and hope the Mexicans would adhere to it. Fannin's men apparently drafted terms of surrender guaranteeing their treatment as prisoners of war, care for the wounded, and ultimately their parole to the United States, but Urrea could not ratify such an agreement. The Mexican general was bound by order of *El Presidente* Santa Anna and by congressional decree to accept no terms other than unconditional surrender. Urrea made it clear to Fannin in person that he could only offer to intercede on the Texans' behalf with Santa Anna and to treat them with respect *until* the government ruled on their fate.

The surviving document of capitulation, a version written in Spanish and signed by Fannin, shows that the Texan commander surrendered his men "subject to the disposition of the supreme government." Fannin apparently did not make this fact clear to his men, since survivor accounts indicate the Texans were led to believe they were surrendering honorably as prisoners of war and would be returned to the United States. But as Urrea recorded in his diary, "Those who assert that I offered guarantees to those who surrendered, speak without knowledge of the facts." De la Peña observed that Urrea's "heart yearned to accord him [Fannin] guarantees that were not within his power to grant, so he limited himself to offering to intercede with the commanding general [Santa Anna], and he kept his word." Although "Fannin and his comrades surrendered with the understanding that their lives would be respected," De la Peña affirmed, "General Urrea had given them no [such] guarantee."

John C. Duval, a witness who later escaped the massacre, provided further insight. "I have always believed myself that Gen. Urrea entered into the capitulation with Col. Fannin in good faith, and that the massacre of the prisoners, which took place some days afterwards, was by the express order of Santa Anna, and against the *remonstrances* of Gen. Urrea. If Gen. Urrea had intended to act treacherously, the massacre, in my opinion, would have taken place as soon as we had delivered up our arms, when we were upon an open prairie, surrounded by a large force of cavalry, where it would have been utterly impossible for a single soul to have escaped, and consequently he could then have given to the world his own version of the affair without fear of contradiction."

Perhaps trying to be optimistic, Fannin was unable to bring himself to tell his men they were really surrendering at the mercy of the government and instead misleadingly assured them of fair treatment. This discrepancy is significant only in light of the ultimate fate of Fannin's command. Although traditional Texan renditions imply some insidious conspiracy in the surrender episode, they assume deceit on Urrea's part but fail to explore Fannin's own unfortunate history of duplicity. For years—even after moving to Texas—Fannin had been involved in the illicit slave trade, illegally shipping and selling Africans in the American Southern states. During the controversy over his Matamoros expedition, which helped split the provisional government, Fannin also deceitfully distorted statements by Governor Henry Smith found in a private letter belonging to his second in command, William Ward, so as to tarnish the character of the governor in the fight within the provisional government. Like Houston, Smith was adamantly opposed to the Matamoros project as folly. Consequently, the libel incident embittered relations between Fannin and Ward. Furthermore, Fannin had emphasized to his allies in the provisional government that they should keep silent on the point of independence for Texas to avoid jeopardizing Mexican Federalist help in the expedition against Matamoros. Additionally, long before the battle of Coleto Fannin's command decisions were criticized by his ranking officers, many of his men, and by Gen. Houston; he had even lost confidence in himself. Writing to Acting Governor Robinson on February 14, Fannin had confessed, "I am not, *practically*, an experienced commander . . . I *know*, if you and the Council do not, that I am incompetent. . . . I do most earnestly ask of you . . . to relieve me, and make a selection of one possessing all the requisites of a commander."

Thus, the enigmatic Fannin enjoyed a reputation neither for integrity nor for sound military judgment and leadership. But to his credit, he "behaved with perfect coolness and self possession" throughout the battle, "and evinced no lack of bravery," according to Dr. Barnard, who was very critical of Fannin's "grievous error in suffering us to stop" in the open prairie. Likewise, De la Peña appraised him: "Although endowed with great courage, which he demonstrated until the moment of death, Fannin also demonstrated his lack of knowledge of the principles of strategy and grand tactics, for otherwise he would have fought while retreating [to the woods], which would have been the best choice."

Following the surrender, some 230 or 240 Texans able to walk were marched back to Goliad. The physicians were made to care for the Mexican wounded to the neglect of their own men. The wounded Texans, including Colonel Fannin who had been hit in the thigh, were transported to Goliad over the next two days. Urrea, meanwhile, continued his advance to secure Guadalupe Victoria, from where he wrote Santa Anna, as he had promised, recommending clemency for the Goliad prisoners. Moving on, he surrounded Ward's men in the Guadalupe woods near "the port known as Linn's House" (Linnville), and accepted the surrender of the dispirited, footsore, and hungry Georgia Battalion on March 22 on the same terms accorded to Fannin. Except for those who escaped en route from Refugio to the Victoria area and those Urrea detained in Victoria as laborers to build boats—which would enable the Mexican army to cross the swollen Guadalupe

River and continue toward Brazoria as planned—Ward and about eighty-five men were marched back to Goliad and imprisoned with Fannin's men in the chapel of Presidio La Bahía, ironically the fort they had so recently commanded. About the same day William P. Miller's Nashville Battalion finally landed at Copano, but was surprised unarmed and taken prisoner without resistance by Urrea's forces then occupying the port. On March 23 they, too, were marched to Goliad and incarcerated, though kept apart from Fannin's men.

Although the battle of Coleto is usually considered meaningful only as a prologue to the massacre, it does have separate significance. While the ultimate story is bound up in the complexity and controversy of the Matamoros expedition,[16] the sequence of events underscores the tragedy of Fannin's inability to make timely decisions crucial for success. This disadvantage was worsened by his disrespect for the capabilities of his enemy and a reluctance, common in the Texas army, to coordinate campaigns. Urrea by contrast showed skill in staying alert to Fannin's plans, keeping the Texans within the presidio an extra day, pursuing and catching them by taking advantage of almost every opportunity, and isolating Ward's men near Victoria while successfully battling Fannin's command at the Coleto. Still, the Texans, though most being untrained, inexperienced volunteers, obeyed their commanders and withstood the onslaught of seasoned enemy troops. The intensity of this protracted battle generated heroism as a commonplace among both sides.

Yet the battle's greatest significance remains fixed to its consequences. Urrea's victories gained him great esteem in the army, but also incurred the jealousy of other generals and especially Santa Anna, who had only recently suffered through victory at the Alamo. These triumphs caused overconfidence among Mexican leaders, who, like Santa Anna, now believed their campaign against the rebellion in Texas to be nearing a successful conclusion. Hence, the greatest consequence of the battle flowed ironically from the pen of the Mexican president himself in the order to execute the Goliad prisoners.

## THE GREAT INFAMY

The Goliad Massacre was not without precedent and *El Presidente* Santa Anna, who ultimately ordered the exterminations, was operating within Mexican law. Therefore, the massacre cannot be considered as isolated from the series of events and legislation preceding it. Santa Anna's chief concern in preparing to subdue the Texas rebellion was the help expected from the United States. An attack on Tampico in November 1835 by Federalist Gen. José Antonio Mexía with men enlisted at New Orleans underscored this factor. The Mexican president ordered twenty-eight survivors of this battle to be tried as pirates; they were convicted and shot on December 14 in what Santa Anna believed would be an effective deterrent to expected help for Texas. He sought and obtained from the Mexican congress the decree of December 30, 1835, which directed that all *foreigners* taken *in arms* against the government should be treated as *pirates*—not prisoners of war—and shot.

In the Texas campaign Santa Anna's main army took no captives. The execution of the murderous December 30 decree fell to Gen. Urrea, whose army took as the first prisoners the survivors of Francis W. Johnson's party in the battle of San Patricio, February 27, 1836. Urrea, according to his esteemed contemporary, Reuben M. Potter, "was not blood thirsty and when not overruled by orders of a superior, or stirred by irritation, was disposed to treat prisoners with lenity." When the general reported to Santa Anna that he had taken prisoners, the president-general ordered him to comply with the decree. Urrea complied to the extent of issuing an order to shoot these prisoners, along with those captured from Grant's party in the battle of Agua Dulce Creek on March 2, but he had no stomach for such cold blooded killing. Thus, when Father Thomas J. Malloy, priest of the Irish colonists, protested the execution, Urrea remitted the men to be imprisoned in Matamoros, asking Santa Anna's pardon for having done so and washing his hands of their fate.

After the battle of Refugio on March 15 Urrea was again confronted with the duty of compliance, when his army captured thirty-three Texans. These included survivors of Amon B. King's company, who had so infuriated their enemy by pursuing and killing local rancheros suspected of aiding Urrea's army. The general satisfied his conscience by ordering King and fourteen of his men shot, while "setting at liberty all who were colonists or Mexicans."

A more difficult situation followed Fannin's capitulation on March 20, owing to the surrender terms, and Ward's surrender of the Georgia Battalion on March 22. Urrea had written Santa Anna from Victoria, as he promised Fannin privately, recommending clemency—a "gesture of generosity after such a hard-fought battle is most worthy of the most singular commendation, and I can do no less than to commend it to your Excellency." He reported nothing in this letter of March 21 about special terms of surrender. On March 23 Santa Anna quickly replied to Urrea's letter by ordering the immediate execution of these "perfidious foreigners," in compliance with the December 30 decree, and repeated the order in a letter on March 24. Meantime, evidently doubting Urrea's willingness to serve as executioner, Santa Anna also sent a direct order on March 23 to the "Officer Commanding the Post of Goliad" to execute immediately the prisoners in his hands, enclosing with this letter a stinging rebuke for the attempt toward mercy and a transcription of "the said decree of the government for your guidance." This order was received about 7:00 P.M., March 26, by Lt. Col. José Nicolás de la Portilla, whom Urrea had left in charge at Goliad. About an hour later Portilla received another order, this one from Urrea, informing him to "treat the prisoners with consideration, and particularly their leader, Fannin," and to employ them in rebuilding Goliad. "What a cruel contrast in these opposite instructions!" Portilla wrote in his diary.

After a restless night Portilla determined that Santa Anna's orders were superior. At sunrise on Palm Sunday, March 27, 1836, he isolated Miller's Nashville Battalion who had been captured without arms and were thus spared. He then formed the unwounded prisoners into three divisions under heavy guard and marched one out on the San Antonio road, another on the Victoria road, and the third along the San Patricio road. The prisoners had little suspicion of their fate, for they had been told a variety of stories, such as how they were to gather wood, drive up cattle, be

Andrew Jackson Houston's *March to the Massacre,* based on contemporary accounts. *Courtesy Center for American History, University of Texas at Austin.*

marched to Matamoros, or even proceed to Copano for passage to New Orleans, as Fannin apparently believed and reported to his men. Thus, their spirits had been raised to singing "Home, Sweet Home" the night before.

At selected spots on each of the three roads, from half to three-fourths of a mile from the presidio, the three divisions were halted. Many of the Texans, as they recognized their fate, fell into despair and cried for mercy. There were some who fought the terror with brave encouragements to their comrades; Robert Fenner called out, "Don't take on so, boys! If we have to die, let's die like brave men!" The guards shot the prisoners at very close range, decimating them. Nearly all were killed at the first fire. Those not killed were pursued with gunfire, bayonet, or lance. The wounded prisoners, having heard the volleys and screams, were then shot to death within the presidio walls. "There was a great contrast in the feelings of the officers and the men," Portilla recorded of his soldiers. "Silence prevailed." Finally, Fannin was led out of the chapel-prison, limping badly from his wound and leaning on Joseph H. Spohn, a member of the Red Rovers spared as a translator. Through Spohn his executioner proclaimed: "For having come with an armed band to commit depredations and revolutionize Texas, the Mexican government is about to chastise you." Fannin

Lt. Col. José Nicolás de la Portilla. *Courtesy Benson Latin American History Collection, University of Texas at Austin.*

"appeared resolute and firm," Spohn recorded of his colonel, who was then shot in the head.

Urrea was outraged and chagrined upon receiving word from Goliad that the exterminations had been carried out, especially since, according to his diary, he had purposefully sent Ward's men to Goliad "to increase the number of the prisoners there in the hope that their very number would save them, for I never thought that the horrible spectacle of that massacre could take place in cold blood and without immediate urgency." De la Peña noted general outrage in the army regarding the criminal immorality of the exterminations. Despite his friendship with Portilla he condemned his "crimes against humanity," noting as well the irony that the "sacrifice" commemorated a holy day in the Passion of Christ—Palm Sunday. De la Peña also denounced his president-general for the scandal, especially because among those shot were colonists who should have enjoyed rights as Mexican citizens rather than being treated, like the foreigners, as pirates. But Santa Anna, in his own rendering of the December 30 decree, declared "on his own that these Mexicans participating in the war had no rights."

Amazingly, twenty-eight men managed to escape. Perhaps the most incredible story was that of William L. Hunter, who was hit by a musket ball; a Mexican soldier, thinking he was not dead, cut his throat, but not deep enough to sever the jugular vein. He was then stabbed with a bayonet and finally beaten about the head with the breech of a musket. Like the others, he was stripped and left for dead. He revived many hours later in the night air, and dragged himself to the San Antonio River to drink and to bind up his wounds. Before daylight he managed to swim the river and eventually sought asylum among local Tejanos he had earlier befriended. His benefactor, a Mexican woman, kept him hidden, nursed, fed, and clothed in a thicket for nearly a week, at which time she supplied him for travel. Hunter eventually made his way to Houston's army.

Another twenty had been spared as physicians, orderlies, translators, or mechanics largely because of the brave and kindly interventions of Col. Francisco Garay and Señora Francisca (Panchita) de Alavez, called the "Angel of Goliad." In addition, Capt. Carlos de la Garza interceded on behalf of at least six Irish colonists caught with Fannin's men who were serving in Hugh Frazer's Refugio militia company. Two physicians, Joseph Barnard and John Shackelford, were taken to San Antonio to treat Mexican wounded from the battle of the Alamo; they later escaped and would publish two of the best original accounts of their ordeal. Shackelford's experience was especially tragic, for among those massacred were two nephews and his oldest son. Portilla wrote that the total number of his prisoners was 445, excluding Miller's Nashville Battalion of 80 men who were separated from the executions. Texas sources specify the number, excluding Miller's men, as 407. This may have been correct. Some of the prisoners taken at Refugio, but not executed with King's men, are known to have been at Goliad, where they were again spared because they were serving the Mexican army as blacksmiths, wheelwrights, and other laborers. The exact fate of others captured at Refugio is not known. They may have been added to the prisoners at Goliad and killed with Fannin on March 27.

Urrea detained about twenty of Ward's men to build boats at Guadalupe Victoria, and Señora de Alavez intervened with her husband, Col. Telésforo Alavez, whom Urrea left in command of the occupation force at Victoria, to spare their lives as well; they afterward escaped. About a week after the Goliad exterminations, Santa Anna ordered the execution of Miller and his men and the others who had been spared at Goliad, but he rescinded the order the next day. The men instead were marched to Matamoros after Houston's victory in the battle of San Jacinto on April 21. Though some managed to escape en route, most remained there until the Mexican government later released them.

The impact of the Goliad Massacre was crucial. Until this episode Santa Anna's reputation had been that of a cunning and crafty man rather than a cruel one. When Fannin's command was finally taken prisoner, Texas had no ample army in the field and the newly created *ad interim* government seemed incapable of forming one. The Texas cause was dependent on the material aid and sympathy of the United States. Had Fannin's and Miller's men been dumped on the wharves at New Orleans, penniless, homesick, humiliated, and distressed, and each with his separate tale of mismanagement and incompetence in the independence movement, the popular Texas cause in the United States most likely would have fallen critically and with it sources of help. But Portilla's volleys at Goliad, together with the fall of the Alamo, branded both Santa Anna and the Mexican people with a reputation for cruelty, aroused the fury of the people of Texas, the United States, and even Great Britain and France. The resulting cry, "Remember the Alamo! Remember Goliad!" contributed immeasurably to Houston's critical victory at San Jacinto and sustaining the independence of the Republic of Texas.

# 5.
# EPILOGUE:
# GHOSTS AND METEORS

AFTER THE EXECUTIONS, THE BODIES of the Texans were poorly burned on piles of green mesquite brush, the remains left exposed to weather, vultures, and coyotes. Following the battle of San Jacinto, Thomas Jefferson Rusk, brigadier general in charge of the Texas army (now numbering an unprecedented 3,000 troops) established his headquarters at Victoria while in pursuit of the retreating Mexican forces. On June 3, 1836, Rusk discovered the grizzly sight at Goliad, gathered the remains, and buried them with military honors. Some of the survivors attended the ceremony. The mass grave remained unmarked. Sometime after San Jacinto the bodies of King's men shot at Refugio were also discovered, buried, and forgotten.

In the first years of the new Republic, the Goliad-Victoria area, having been directly in the war zone, was virtually deserted. Many of the Hispanic citizens retreated south with the Mexican army, or like the De León family (including Carbajal and Benavides), were forced to flee by the Texas army and incoming Anglo-American settlers bearing bitter prejudice against all Mexicans, even Tejanos that had supported the Texas cause. The sons and sons-in-law of Martín De León had contributed loyal service and a fortune in horses, mules, cattle, military equipment, and provisions to the Texas army, offering as well the safety of their ranches to colonists needing refuge. Singled out first as traitors by the Mexican army and then victimized by newcomers, their story is one of the great but obscure tragedies of the revolution. Goliad County, like Victoria County, became one of the twenty-three original counties created by the First Congress of the Republic of Texas in 1836; but resettlement was slow. Even by 1850 Goliad County recorded a population of less than 650 people.

Racial strife and Indian attacks kept things troubled, notably the Great Comanche Raid of 1840, which especially terrorized Victoria and destroyed Linnville. As Federalists in northern Mexico continued to battle Santa Anna's Centralist policies, Goliad, Victoria, Refugio, San Patricio, and San Antonio were again pulled into the Mexican orbit as recruiting and supply stations for the Federalist cause. Various reinvasions by Mexican Centralists—the most famous being Gen. Adrian Woll's expedition of 1842—singled out and attacked these settlements, exacerbating the turmoil of the times. Philip Dimmitt, whom the Mexican government considered particularly notorious for having been among the first to proclaim independence at Goliad and who had continued to sell goods to Federalist suppliers, was captured by one of these invading armies and imprisoned at Agua Nueva, Mexico, where he died. Texan counterattacks against these invasions were also recruited and supplied from these same towns.[17] By the mid-1840s Victoria, with a growing Anglo-American and German population, emerged as the commercial center for the area, eclipsing its sister communities of Goliad, Gonzales, and Refugio.

Meanwhile, on January 12, 1841, the congress of the Republic of Texas recognized the ownership of the Catholic Church of old Mission La Bahía, then mostly in ruins, though the church failed to get possession of it. After Texas statehood, these ruins were used by Hillyer Female College, a Baptist institution established in 1848, and later by Aranama College, founded in 1856 under the auspices of the Presbyterian Church. As for the presidio, American soldiers discharged after the Mexican War of 1846–1848 damaged the already decaying structure. Still, from 1846 to about 1854 Judge Pryor Lea, a notable public official and railroad promoter, used the presidio chapel, still intact, as a residence and the old parade ground as an experimental garden. Frederick Law

Olmstead, who toured the area and described its awful poverty and ruination in *A Journey Through Texas* (1857), found the chapel still occupied. About 1855 the Catholic Church reestablished its ownership of Presidio La Bahía and began conducting services there.

On March 24, 1931, the city of Goliad and Goliad County transferred the long dilapidated Mission La Bahía to the state, which agreed to preserve it as a historic park. During Franklin D. Roosevelt's New Deal (1933–1941), federal public works projects conducted archaeological, historical, and architectural research at the site. Its buildings were then restored with local Civilian Conservation Corps labor under the supervision of the National Park Service and the University of Texas. Additional reconstruction occurred in the 1960s, and by 1987 the mission appeared as it had in 1749. Listed in the National Register of Historic Places, the beautifully restored mission is the focus of Goliad State Historical Park and is administered by the Texas Department of Parks and Wildlife.

The chapel of Presidio La Bahía was also restored as a New Deal public works project, and in 1936 the structure was recorded in the Historic American Buildings Survey. At the urging of Bishop Mariano Simón Garriga, and with permission of the Catholic bishop of Corpus Christi, the entire presidio was reconstructed from stuccoed limestone between 1963 and 1967, with funds from the Kathryn O'Connor Foundation and under the direction of architect-restorer Raiford Stripling and archaeologist Roland E. Beard, who had also supervised the mission restoration. The fort was rebuilt in accord with an old picture by a New York lithographer and with use of the notes and map drawn by Joseph M. Chadwick, Fannin's topographical engineer and supervisor of fortifications. The evacuations revealed nine layers of previous occupation and thousands of artifacts, now on display in the museum located in the restored officers' quarters. The restoration is praised as one of the most authentic in the United States and as the finest example of a presidio now extant. Lady Bird Johnson, in her role as first lady, together with Kathryn O'Connor, dedicated the presidio as a Registered National Historic Landmark in 1967.

The presidio also houses an archive-museum relating to the exploration, settlement, and development of Texas and the Catholic Church. Owned and operated by the Catholic Diocese of Victoria, the site is closely associated with Goliad State Historical Park. Annual Cinco de Mayo celebrations are held honoring the birthplace of Ignacio Zaragoza, and since the Texas Sesquicentennial (1985–1986), the Crossroads of Texas Living History Association periodically reenacts various episodes in the presidio's eventful life. The public is invited to become members in the "Friends of the Fort," which helps preserve and promote the presidio's history. Holy Mass is celebrated every Sunday in the beautiful presidio chapel—where the Goliad Declaration of Independence was signed and where Fannin's men were held prisoner before execution—with a major festival being held on December 10, the feast day of Our Lady of Loreto.

The earlier sites of presidio and mission La Bahía in Victoria County have also been examined by historians and archaeologists; unearthed artifacts are displayed at the Goliad museums. These sites are listed in the National Register of Historic Places and marked with small monuments. The ruins of Mission Rosario, six miles west of Goliad on U.S. Hwy. 59, became part of Goliad State Historical Park in 1971. A large monument at Fannin Battleground State Historic Site, nine miles east of Goliad on U.S. Hwy. 59 at the town of Fannin, marks the location of the battle of Coleto.

The mass grave of Fannin's men remained unmarked until about 1858, when a Goliad merchant, George Von Dohlen, placed a pile of rocks on what was believed to be the site. In April 1885 a memorial was finally erected (but in the city of Goliad rather than on the burial site) by the Fannin Monument Association, formed by William L. Hunter, a massacre survivor. In 1930 some Goliad Boy Scouts found charred bone fragments that had been unearthed over the years by gophers, and an excursion to the site by Goliad residents on New Year's Day, 1932, succeeded in attracting an investigation of the site by University of Texas anthropologist J. E. Pearce. The authenticity of the grave site was further verified by historians Clarence R. Wharton and Harbert Davenport. In 1936, in celebration of the Texas Centennial, money

The Fannin Memorial Monument, Goliad. *Courtesy Texas Department of Transportation.*

was appropriated to build a massive pink granite "Heroes at Rest" monument, which displays the names of all the known dead. The monument was dedicated on June 4, 1939, with Harbert Davenport presenting the address, which was published as "The Men of Goliad" in the *Southwestern Historical Quarterly* (1939). The unmarked grave of King's men was discovered by accident on May 9, 1934. The bones were identified, and on June 17, 1934, they were reinterred in Mount Calvary Catholic Cemetery near Refugio. For the Centennial in 1936 the state of Texas erected two memorials to King and his men, one in Refugio and another at the grave site.

It seems fitting to end this story with controversy. It is well-known among locals that there are eerie happenings at Goliad's old presidio. Credible but fearful witnesses corroborate sightings and occurrences bound neither by day or night—a ghostly friar in a hooded black robe praying in Latin while wandering the quadrangle; a woman wearing white drifting over a grave that produces the sounds of crying babies; the voice of an woman singing beautifully in soprano (the witness was there alone); the sound of haunting church music accompanied by a woman's humming; a lady dressed in black and wearing a veil is seen sobbing in the chapel by the candles, then vanishes; the singing of an unseen women's choir seeming to come from the walls of the fort. Skeptics abound, but the ghosts of Goliad persistently find their haunts among presidio workers, townsfolk, visitors, and in the newspapers reporting the events.

Back in 1891 the heavens gave birth to a most appropriate metaphor for the historical Goliad. A large meteor, said to be "about the size of a whisky barrel," streaked through the atmosphere and landed near the Coleto battlefield at Fannin. (As late as the 1950s folks recalled that the meteorite was still on display at Fannin Battleground Park.) "Excitement was high," a local paper disclosed. Residents were said to fear that the world was coming to an end. "Everybody in our city knows all about it," a reporter wrote, "and each one tells a different yarn. So many different mouths are being shot off and so many different tails are wagging that your correspondent can't tell what to believe." Indeed.

# SUGGESTED READING

THERE IS A WEALTH OF PUBLISHED SOURCES for readers desiring further study of La Bahía's rich heritage. Always the starting place for biographies, events, towns, and innumerable topics in Texas history is Walter Prescott Webb, H. Bailey Carroll, and Eldon Stephen Branda (eds.), *Handbook of Texas* (Austin: Texas State Historical Association, 1952, 1976), currently in three volumes but forthcoming in a completely revised and greatly expanded multi-volume, illustrated edition. The Association also publishes the *Southwestern Historical Quarterly*, which likewise enjoys an enviable reputation for scholarship in Texas history. Informative single-volume overviews include T. R. Fehrenbach, *Lone Star: A History of Texas and the Texans* (New York: Macmillan, 1968); James L. Haley, *Texas: From the Frontier to Spindletop* (New York: St. Martin's Press, 1985); David Nevin and the Editors of Time-Life Books, *The Old West: The Texans* (New York: Time-Life Books, 1975); and Rupert N. Richardson, Ernest Wallace, and Adrian Anderson, *Texas: The Lone Star State* (Englewood Cliffs, N.J.: Prentice-Hall, 1981).

Commendable studies of general periods or topics relevant to Goliad include Herbert Bolton, *Texas in the Middle Eighteenth Century* (1915; reprint, Austin: University of Texas Press, 1970); Carlos E. Castañeda, *Our Catholic Heritage in Texas* (1936–1958; reprint, New York: Arno, 1976); the volumes in the Seymour V. Connor (ed.), *The Saga of Texas* Series, especially Odie B. Faulk, *A Successful Failure, 1519–1810*; and David M. Vigness, *The Revolutionary Decades, 1810–1836* (Austin: Steck-Vaughn, 1965). Helpful still are the vintage overviews of Herbert Howe Bancroft, *History of the North Mexican States and Texas* (San Francisco: The History Co., 1889); Henry Stuart Foote, *Texas and the Texans* (1841; reprint, Austin: The Steck Co., 1935); Frank W. Johnson and Eugene C. Barker, *History of Texas and Texans, 1799–1884* (New York: American Historical Society, 1914); Dudley Goodall Wooten (ed.), *A Comprehensive History of Texas, 1685–1897* (1898; reprint, Austin: Texas State Historical Association, 1986); Louis J. Wortham, *A History of Texas from Wilderness to Commonwealth* (Fort Worth: Wortham-Molyneaux Co., 1935); and Henderson K. Yoakum, *History of Texas from Its First Settlement in 1680 to Its Annexation to the United States in 1846* (New York: J. S. Redfield, 1855). See also *Diccionário Porrúa de Historia, Biografía, y Geografía de México* (Mexico: Editorial Porrua, SA, 1964); and *Suplemento* (Mexico, 1966), for Mexican biographies.

Comprehensive sources for the Goliad-Victoria-Refugio area are Roy Grimes (ed.), *300 Years in Victoria County* (1968; reprint, Austin: Nortex, 1985); Keith Guthrie, *Texas Forgotten Ports: Mid-Gulf Coast Ports from Corpus Christi to Matagorda Bay* (Austin: Eakin Press, 1988); *The Handbook of Victoria County*, comp. Staff of the *Handbook of Texas* (Austin: Texas State Historical Association, 1990); Hobart Huson, *Refugio: A Comprehensive History of Refugio County from Aboriginal Times to 1953* (Woodsboro, Tex.: Rooke Foundation, 1953, 1955); Victor Marion Rose, *Some Historical Facts in Regard to the Settlement of Victoria, Texas* (Laredo, Tex.: *Daily Times* Press, 1883; reprinted as *A Republication of . . . Victor Rose's History of Victoria*, ed. J. W. Petty Jr. and Kate Stoner O'Connor [Victoria, Tex.: Book Mart, 1961]); and Abel Rubio, *Stolen Heritage: The Lost Becerra Grant in Texas* (Austin: Eakin-Sunbelt, 1986).

Spanish-era topical treatments appropriate to Goliad and Victoria include Herbert E. Bolton, "The Founding of Mission Rosario: A Chapter in the History of the Gulf Coast," *Quarterly of the Texas State Historical Association*, X (Oct., 1906); Herbert E. Bolton, "The Location of La Salle's Colony on the Gulf of Mexico," *Mississippi*

*Valley Historical Review,* II (Sept., 1915); Elaine Bostic, "La Bahía: The Forgotten Fortress," *Texas Highways* (Mar., 1968); Eleanor Claire Buckley, "The Aguayo Expedition into Texas and Louisiana, 1719–1722," *Quarterly of the Texas State Historical Association,* XV (1911–1912); Donald E. Chipman, *Spanish Texas, 1519–1821* (Austin: University of Texas Press, 1992); Julia Kathryn Garret, *Green Flag Over Texas* (New York and Dallas: Cordova Press, 1939); Charles Wilson Hackett, "The Marquis of San Miguel de Aguayo and His Recovery of Texas from the French," *Southwestern Historical Quarterly,* LIX (1945–1946); H. M. Henderson, "The Magee-Gutiérrez Expedition," *Southwestern Historical Quarterly,* LX (1951–1952); Lawrence Francis Hill, *José de Escandón and the Founding of Nuevo Santander* (Columbus: Ohio State University Press, 1926); Jack Jackson, *Los Mesteños: Spanish Ranching in Texas, 1721–1821* (College Station: Texas A&M University Press, 1986); Benedict Leutenegger and Marion A. Habig, *The Zacatecan Missionaries in Texas, 1716–1834* (Austin: Texas Historical Survey Committee, 1973); *Mission Espíritu Santo: Exploring the Past* (Austin: Texas Department of Parks and Wildlife, 1978); William H. Oberste, *History of the Refugio Mission* (Refugio, Tex.: Timely Remarks, 1942); Thomas P. O'Rourke, *The Franciscan Missions in Texas, 1690–1793* (1927; reprint, New York: AMS Press, 1974); Charles Ramsdell, "Espíritu Santo: An Early Texas Cattle Ranch," *Texas Geographic Magazine,* XIII (Fall, 1949); Charles Ramsdell, Spanish Goliad, MS., National Park Service, 1936–1937 (Washington, D.C.: National Archives); Tommy Pinkard, "Return to Goliad," *Texas Highways,* (May, 1978); Paul H. Walters, "Secularization of the La Bahía Missions," *Southwestern Historical Quarterly,* LIV (Jan., 1951); Robert S. Weddle, *Wilderness Manhunt: The Spanish Search for La Salle* (Austin: University of Texas Press, 1973); and Theodore Lawrence White, "Marquis de Rubí's Inspection of the Eastern Presidios on the Northern Frontier of New Spain" (Ph.D. diss., University of Texas, 1953).

For colonial and revolutionary Goliad and Victoria see Eugene C. Barker, *The Life of Stephen F. Austin, Founder of Texas, 1793–1836: A Chapter in the Westward Movement of the Anglo-American People* (reprint, Austin: Texas State Historical Association, 1949); Alwyn

Barr, *Texans in Revolt: The Battle for San Antonio, 1835* (Austin: University of Texas Press, 1990); William C. Binkley, *The Texas Revolution* (Baton Rouge: Louisiana State University Press, 1952); Harbert Davenport, "King and Ward at Refugio," *Southwestern Historical Quarterly*, IL (Apr., 1946); Harbert Davenport, "Men of Goliad," *Southwestern Historical Quarterly*, XLIII (July, 1939); Joe Tom Davis, *Legendary Texians* (Austin: Eakin Press, 1982–1986); Robert S. Davis Jr., "Goliad and the Georgia Battalion: Georgia Participation in the Texas Revolution," *Journal of Southwest Georgia History*, IV (Fall, 1986); Arnoldo De León, *They Called Them Greasers* (Austin: University of Texas Press, 1983); Arnoldo De León, "Tejanos and the Texas War for Independence: Historiography's Judgement," *New Mexico Historical Review*, LXI (Apr., 1986); Roy Grimes, *Goliad 130 Years After* (Victoria, Tex.: Victoria *Advocate* Publishing Co., 1966); Claude Elliott, "Alabama and the Texas Revolution," *Southwestern Historical Quarterly*, L (Jan., 1947); Irene Hohmann Friedrichs, *History of Goliad* (Victoria, Tex.: Regal Printers, 1961); A. B. J. Hammett, *The Empresario Don Martín De León* (Waco: Texian Press, 1973); Rachel B. Hébert, *The Forgotten Colony: San Patricio de Hibernia* (Burnet, Tex.: Eakin Press, 1981); Andrew Jackson Houston, *Texas Independence* (Houston: Anson Jones Press, 1938); Hobart Huson, *Captain Phillip Dimmitt's Commandancy of Goliad, 1835–1836* (Austin: Von Boeckmann-Jones, 1974); Hobart Huson, *El Cópano: Ancient Port of Béxar and La Bahía* (Refugio, Tex.: Refugio *Timely Remarks*, 1935); Paul D. Lack, *The Texas Revolutionary Experience: A Political and Social History, 1835-1836* (College Station: Texas A&M University Press, 1992); Edward A. Lukes, *DeWitt Colony of Texas* (Austin: Jenkins Publishing Co., Pemberton Press, 1976); Ohland Morton, *Terán and Texas* (Austin: Texas State Historical Association, 1948); William H. Oberste, *"Remember Goliad"* (Austin: Von Boeckmann-Jones, 1949); William H. Oberste, *Texas Irish Empresarios and Their Colonies: Power & Hewetson; Mullen & McGloin* (Austin: Von Boeckmann-Jones, 1953); Kathryn Stoner O'Connor, *The Presidio La Bahía del Espíritu Santo de Zúñiga, 1721 to 1846* (Austin: Von Boeckmann-Jones, 1966); Jakie L. Pruett and Everett B. Cole Sr., *Goliad Massacre: A Tragedy of the Texas Revolution* (Austin: Eakin Press, 1985); Ethel Zivley Rather, "DeWitt's

Colony," *Quarterly of the Texas State Historical Association*, VIII (Oct., 1904); James M. Robertson, "Captain Amon B. King," *Southwestern Historical Quarterly*, XXIX (Oct., 1925); Richard G. Santos, *Santa Anna's Campaign Against Texas, 1835–1836* (Waco: Texian Press, 1968); Jewel Davis Scarborough, "The Georgia Battalion in the Texas Revolution: A Critical Study," *Southwestern Historical Quarterly*, LXIII (Apr., 1960); Goldie Capers Smith, "Georgia's Gift to Texas: The Lone Star Flag," *Georgia Review*, XIX (1965); Ruby Cumby Smith, "James W. Fannin, Jr., in the Texas Revolution," *Southwestern Historical Quarterly*, XXIII (Oct., 1919, Jan., Apr., 1920); David J. Weber, *The Mexican Frontier, 1821–1846: The American Southwest Under Mexico* (Albuquerque: University of New Mexico Press, 1982); Clarence Wharton, *Remember Goliad* (Houston: McCurdy-Young, 1931). See also Harbert Davenport, An Unfinished Study of Fannin and His Men, MS., Center for American History, University of Texas at Austin; Hobart Huson, Colonel Fannin's Execution of Gen. Houston's Orders to Evacuate Goliad, MS., Center for American History, University of Texas at Austin; and Austin colonist Noah Smithwick's personal recollections in *The Evolution of a State; or, Recollections of Old Texas Days* (Austin: Gammel Book Co., 1900). See additionally the biographical treatments in Randolph B. Campbell, *Sam Houston and the American Southwest* (New York: HarperCollins, 1993); Llerena B. Friend, *Sam Houston: The Great Designer* (Austin: University of Texas Press, 1954); M. K. Wisehart, *Sam Houston: American Giant* (Washington, D.C.: Robert B. Luce, 1962); Archie P. McDonald, *Travis* (Austin: Pemberton Press, 1976); and Joseph Milton Nance, *Heroes of Texas* (Waco: Texian Press, 1966). See also "Gophers Unearth Charred Remains of Fannin's Men," Victoria *Advocate*, Jan. 3, 1932.

Comprehensive collections of first-hand accounts bearing on the Goliad-Victoria orbit are Eugene C. Barker (ed.), *The Austin Papers* (3 vols.; Washington, D.C.: U.S. Government Printing Office, 1924–1928); Eugene C. Barker and Amelia W. Williams (eds.), *The Writings of Sam Houston* (8 vols.; Austin: University of Texas Press, 1938–1943); John Henry Brown, *History of Texas from 1685 to 1892* (1892; reprint, Austin: Jenkins Publishing Co., 1970); William C.

Binkley (ed.), *Official Correspondence of the Texas Revolution, 1835–1836* (New York: D. Appleton-Century, 1936); H. P. N. Gammel (comp.), *The Laws of Texas*, Vol. 1, *1822–1837* . . . (Austin: Gammel Book Co., 1898); Charles Adams Gulick Jr., Harriet Smither, et al. (eds.), *The Papers of Mirabeau Buonaparte Lamar* (6 vols.; 1921–1927; reprint, Austin: Pemberton Press, 1968); Wade Houston (comp.), *David G. Burnet Letters* (La Grange, Tex.: La Grange *Journal*, 1944); Hobart Huson (comp.), Reporting Texas [collection of accounts published in Kentucky and Ohio newspapers not available elsewhere], MS., Center for American History, University of Texas at Austin; John Holmes Jenkins (ed.), *The Papers of the Texas Revolution, 1835–1836* (10 vols.; Austin: Presidial Press, 1973); Virginia Houston Taylor, *The Spanish Archives of the General Land Office of Texas* (Austin: Lone Star Press, 1955); and Ernest Wallace and David Vigness (eds.), *Documents of Texas History* (Austin: The Steck Co. 1960).

Spanish-era first-hand accounts relating to La Bahía are Joaquín de Arredondo, "Joaquín de Arredondo's Report on the Battle of the Medina," ed. Mattie Austin Hatcher, *Southwestern Historical Quarterly*, XI (Jan., 1908); Jean Louis Berlandier, *The Indians of Texas in 1830*, ed. John C. Ewers (Washington, D.C.: Smithsonian Institution Press, 1969; Juan Antonio de la Peña, *Peña's Diary of the Aguayo Expedition*, trans. Peter P. Forrestal (Preliminary Studies of the Texas Catholic Historical Association 2.7 [Jan., 1935]); Charles W. Hackett (ed.), *Pichardo's Treatise on the Limits of Louisiana and Texas* (Austin: University of Texas Press, 1931–1946); Fray Damián Massanet, "Carta de Don Damián Massanet a Don Carlos de Siguenze Sobre el Descubrimiento de la Bahía del Espíritu Santo," *Quarterly of the Texas State Historical Association*, II (Apr., 1899); Juan Agustín Morfi, *History of Texas, 1673–1779*, trans. Carlos E. Castañeda (Albuquerque: Quivira Society, 1935); Juan Augustín Morfi, *Indian Excerpts*, trans. Frederick C. Chabot (San Antonio: Naylor, 1931); Domingo Ramón, *Captain Don Domingo Ramón's Diary of His Expedition into Texas in 1716*, trans. Paul J. Foik (Preliminary Studies of the Texas Catholic Historical Society 2.5 [Apr., 1933]); and Fray Gaspar José de Solís, *The Solís Diary of 1767, Father*

*Fray José de Solís,* ed. Peter R. Forestal (Preliminary Studies of the Texas Catholic Historical Society 1.6 [1931]). See also Henry Putney Beers, *Spanish and Mexican Records of the American Southwest: A Bibliographic Guide to Archive and Manuscript Sources* (Tucson: University of Arizona Press, 1979).

Mexican first-hand accounts for the revolutionary period appropriate to Goliad are José Enrique de la Peña, *With Santa Anna in Texas: A Personal Narrative of the Revolution,* trans. and ed. Carmen Perry, intro. by Llerena Friend (College Station: Texas A&M University Press, 1975); Vicente Filisola, *Memorias para la historia de la guerra de Tejas* (México, D.F., 1848, 1849), trans. by Wallace Woolsey, *Memoirs for the History of the War in Texas* (Austin: Eakin Press, 1985, 1987); Antonio López de Santa Anna, *The Eagle: The Autobiography of Santa Anna,* ed. Ann Fears Crawford (1967; reprint, Austin: State House Press, 1988); Antonio López de Santa Anna, *Manifiesto que de sus Operaciones en la Campaña de Tejas* (1837), trans. Carlos E. Castañeda in *The Mexican Side of the Texas Revolution* (2nd ed.; Austin: Graphic Ideas, 1970); and José Urrea, *Diario de las Operaciones Miltares de la Division que al Mando del General José Urrea Hizo la Campaña de Tejas* (1838), trans. Carlos E. Castañeda in *The Mexican Side of the Texas Revolution* (1970). Excerpts of the diary of José Nicolás de la Portilla and other Mexican officers are in Urrea's account in Castañeda, *Mexican Side of the Texas Revolution.* See also José Sánchez Garza, *La Rebelión de Texas,* vol. 2, *Manucrito inédito de 1836 por un oficial de Santa Anna* (Mexico City, 1955); and Genaro García, *Documentos inéditos o muy raros para la historia de Mexico: Antonio López de Santa Anna [et al]* (Mexico: Editorial Porrúa, S. A., 1974).

Published accounts among Texan participants in the Goliad campaigns of 1835 and 1836 include Charles H. Ayers, "Lewis T. Ayers," *Quarterly of the Texas State Historical Association,* IX (Apr., 1906); Dr. Joseph H. Barnard, *Dr. J. H. Barnard's Journal: A Composite of Known Versions of the Journal of Dr. Joseph H. Barnard,* ed. Hobart Huson (Refugio, Tex. [?]: n.p., 1949); Andrew Michael Boyle, "Reminiscences of the Texas Revolution," *Southwestern Historical Quarterly,* XIII (Apr., 1910); Samuel T. Brown, "Fannin's Massacre—Account of the Georgia Battalion," in *A Texas Scrap-*

*Book,* comp. DeWitt Clinton Baker (1875; reprint, Austin: Steck Co., 1935); Dilliard Cooper, "Account of His Escape from the Goliad Massacre," ed. Fannie A. D. Darden, in Colorado [Texas] *Citizen,* July 30, 1874; William Corner, "John Crittenden Duval: The Last Survivor of the Goliad Massacre," *Quarterly of the Texas State Historical Association,* I (July, 1897); Jesús (Comanche) Cuellar, "Captain Jesús Cuellar, Texas Cavalry, Otherwise 'Comanche,'" ed. Harbert Davenport, *Southwestern Historical Quarterly,* XXX (1926–1927); Donald Day and Harry Ullom (eds.), *The Autobiography of Sam Houston* (Norman: University of Oklahoma Press, 1954); John C. Duval, *Early Times in Texas, or the Adventures of Jack Dobell,* ed. Mabel Major and Rebecca W. Smith (1892; new ed., Lincoln: University of Nebraska Press, 1986); Hermann Ehrenberg, *With Milam and Fannin: Adventures of a German Boy in Texas' Revolution;* trans. Charlotte Churchill (Austin: Pemberton Press, 1968); Dr. Joseph E. Field, *Three Years in Texas, Including a View of the Texan Revolution* (1836); Douglas D. Hale Jr., "Gustav Bunsen: A German Rebel in the Texas Revolution," *East Texas Historical Journal,* VI (Oct. 1968); Lester Hamilton, *Goliad Survivor Isaac D. Hamilton* (San Antonio: Naylor, 1971); William Kennedy, *Texas: The Rise, Progress, and Prospects of the Republic of Texas* (London: R. Hastings, 1841); John J. Linn, *Reminiscences of Fifty Years in Texas* (1883; reprint, Austin: State House Books, 1986); Abel Morgan, *An Account of the Battle of Goliad and Fanning's [sic] Massacre: And the Capture and Imprisonment of Abel Morgan, Written by Himself* (1847 [?]; reprint in Kathryn Stoner O'Connor, *The Presidio La Bahía del Espíritu Santo de Zúñiga, 1721–1846* [Austin: Von Boeckmann-Jones, 1966]); Elizabeth McAnulty Owens, *Elizabeth McAnulty Owens, the Story of Her Life* (San Antonio: Naylor, 1936); L. T. Pease, "Narrative of Ward's Battle," in *Texas and the Texans,* Vol. 2, by Henry Stuart Foote (1841; reprint, Austin: Steck Co., 1935); John E. Roller, "Capt. John Sowers Brooks," *Quarterly of the Texas State Historical Association,* IX (Oct., 1905); Dr. John Shackelford, "Some Few Notes upon a Part of the Texas War," in Foote, *Texas and the Texans,* Vol. 2; Roy W. Smith, "The Quarrel between Governor Smith and the Council of the Provisional Government of the Republic," *Quarterly of the Texas State Historical Association,* V (Apr., 1902); and Joseph H.

Spohn, "Massacre of Fannin's Men," account in Gulick et al., *Lamar Papers* (1968).

For Goliad and Victoria's troubled years during the early republic see Donaly E. Brice, *The Great Comanche Raid: Boldest Indian Attack of the Texas Republic* (Austin: Eakin Press, 1987); Joseph Milton Nance, *After San Jacinto: The Texas-Mexican Frontier, 1836–1841* (Austin: University of Texas Press, 1963); and Joseph Milton Nance, *Attack and Counterattack: The Texas Mexican Frontier, 1842* (Austin: University of Texas Press, 1964).

# NOTES

1. Bustillo served as captain of Presidio La Bahía from 1724 to 1731, and was so successful an administrator that he was appointed governor of Texas, 1731–1734, and then served in the government of Mexico City. In 1751 he was a member of the Audiencia, the highest judicial and administrative body of New Spain.

2. Also known as Nuestra Señora del Rosario de los Cujanes, this mission was established in 1754 near the San Antonio River in the vicinity of Espíritu Santo to minister to the various Karankawan tribes, especially the Cujanes. Though now in ruins, the site is designated by historical marker and located four miles west of present Goliad.

3. Published in 1772 in Madrid as *Reglamento e Instrucción para los Presidos que se han de formar en la Línea de Frontera de la Nueva España*.

4. The Piguiques were probably Coahuiltecan but later associated with Karankawan tribes. The Manos de Perro, meaning "dog feet" in Spanish, were coastal Coahuiltecans.

5. This was the last mission established in Spanish Texas. Founded in 1793 near the convergence of the San Antonio and Guadalupe Rivers, it was moved in late 1794 to the Mission River site because of unhealthy climate. Like its sister missions Espíritu Santo and Rosario, Mission Refugio was launched by Franciscans of the college of Nuestra Señora de Guadalupe de Zacatecas, although specifically for ministry to Karankawan tribes.

6. Nolan, an Irish-born Kentuckian, visited La Bahía during his horse trading expeditions to Texas throughout the 1790s. His activities in East Texas, which raised enough Spanish suspicions to order his arrest, and which ended in his death on March 4, 1801, indirectly involved Presidio La Bahía. The garrison was put on alert under Francisco Amangual, who escorted Nolan's captured companions to Saltillo, Mexico.

7. Citizens of Texas of Mexican descent.

8. This terrible disease greatly reduced the population of Goliad, Guadalupe Victoria, Gonzales, and especially the Power and Hewetson colony. The titles for

Manchola's land grants were issued to his widow, María Jesús De León, in October 1833, indicating that the Goliad alcalde also died in this epidemic. The widow De León also received grants in her father's colony and in the Power and Hewetson colony, making her one of the large land owners of the region.

9. "Centralist" and "Federalist" describe the opposing factions in Mexico regarding either loyalty to Santa Anna's policies and government (centralism) or loyalty to the Constitution of 1824 (federalism). Most Federalists were in the northern provinces, especially Coahuila y Texas. Initially, most Texans (Anglos and Tejanos) supported the Federalist cause and sought to remain Mexican citizens, despite the political campaign to separate Coahuila and Texas into two states. Thus, Texans would find allies in their sister northern provinces to resist Santa Anna. Eventually, an independence movement in Texas overshadowed this internal federalism-centralism conflict, launching a campaign to free Texas from the Mexican orbit altogether.

10. Now Lipantitlán State Historic Site.

11. Grant served in the legislature of Coahuila y Texas, participated in the siege of Béxar, and was elected as a Goliad delegate to the Consultation at San Felipe but did not leave the army to attend. His most remembered role was with Francis W. Johnson in organizing an expedition against Matamoros.

12. Many serving the Texas cause in 1836 were American volunteers and not Texas colonists having Mexican citizenship; most of Fannin's command, for example, were Americans—especially from Georgia, Alabama, and Louisiana. I use the term "Texan," however, to denote those fighting for independence.

13. The first Texas Congress adopted this Lone Star flag as the official banner and sent some of Santa Anna's captured silver service to Johanna Troutman in appreciation. She died in Georgia in 1879. In 1913 Texas Governor O. B. Colquitt secured permission to have her remains brought to Texas for interment in the State Cemetery, where a bronze statue was erected as a monument to her memory. Her portrait hangs in the Senate chamber of the Texas state capitol.

14. The Mobile Greys, originally organized by James Butler Bonham and Albert C. Horton in Alabama, were reorganized in San Antonio for the Matamoros expedition, ultimately becoming part of Fannin's LaFayette Battalion.

15. Originally named "*la Batala del Encinal del Perdido*," or the "Battle of the Oak Grove of the Perdido [Creek]," it also has been called the battle of the Plain of Perdido, the battle of the Prairie, the battle of Goliad, and Fannin's Defeat.

16. The Matamoros expedition of 1835–1836 must be regarded as one of the most disastrous components of the Texas Revolution. It brought to crisis the rift between the governor and the council and paralyzed the provisional government. It left the Texas forces divided as to purpose. It shows that the Texans discounted reports warning of Santa Anna's approaching armies, while relying on rumors of great numbers of volunteers arriving from the United States and, more importantly, massive support by Federalists in the Mexican interior. Thus, the expedition proved a major factor in the events leading to the defeat of Texan forces at the Alamo, San Patricio, Agua Dulce Creek, Refugio, Coleto Creek, and hence the Goliad Massacre.

17. The most tragic of these was the ill-fated Mier Expedition of 1842, which resulted in the infamous Black Bean Episode at Salado, Mexico, on March 25, 1843. Seventeen of the 176 captured Texans were chosen by lottery and shot—including John L. Cash of Victoria, whose brother, George W. Cash, had been executed in the Goliad Massacre.

## ABOUT THE AUTHOR

Craig H. Roell is a native of Victoria, Texas. After completing degrees from the Victoria College and the University of Houston, he earned the M.A. and Ph.D. at the University of Texas at Austin. He has authored a variety of books and articles. He was a scholar-in-residence—Nelda C. and H. J. Lutcher Stark Foundation Fellow in Texas Studies—for the Texas State Historical Association's revised *Handbook of Texas* project, South Texas Division. He was the major contributor to the Texas State Historical Association's *The Handbook of Victoria County* (1990). He has also published *The Piano in America, 1890–1940* (1989; rpt. 1991); *Lyndon B. Johnson: A Bibliography, Volume 2* (1988); *William McKinley: A Bibliography*, with Lewis L. Gould (1988); "The Development of Tin Pan Alley" in *America's Musical Pulse*, edited by Kenneth J. Bindas (1992); "The Piano in the American Home," in *The Arts and the American Home, 1890–1930*, edited by Jessica H. Foy and Karal Ann Marling (1994); and additional pieces in books, encyclopedias, and journals. Dr. Roell has taught at the Ohio State University and is a professor of economic and cultural history at Georgia Southern University, Statesboro.

9

57 30